REACHING FOR THE STARS

KEVIN COSTNER
AWARD-WINNING ACTOR/DIRECTOR

Written By: Sue L. Hamilton

Published by Abdo & Daughters, 6535 Cecilia Circle, Edina, Minnesota 55439.

Library bound edition distributed by Rockbottom Books, Pentagon Tower, P.O. Box 36036, Minneapolis, Minnesota 55435.

Copyright © 1991 by Abdo Consulting Group, Inc., Pentagon Tower, P.O. Box 36036, Minneapolis, Minnesota 55435. International copyrights reserved in all countries. No part of this book may be reproduced in any form without written permission from the publisher. Printed in the United States.

Library of Congress Number: ISBN: 1-56239-087-2

Cover Photo by: Reuters/Bettmann
Inside Photos by: AP/Wide World Photos - Pgs. 4,7,10,11,12,13,15,17,18,21,25,28,31
                 Reuters/Bettmann - Pgs. 23, 30

Edited By: John C. Hamilton

TABLE OF CONTENTS

A Shooting Star—Bow 'n Arrows & Six-Guns 5

Baseball, Business or Acting? 6

Playing Dead: *The Big Chill* 8

Touching Success 10

Fielding His Dreams 13

Directing *"Dances"* 16

Troubleshooting in England 24

Star Status 29

Kevin Costner's Address 32

Kevin Costner in his role as Lt. John Dunbar in Dances with Wolves.

A SHOOTING STAR
BOW 'N ARROWS & SIX-GUNS

Only days after completing the shooting of *Dances with Wolves*, his three-hour Western epic, Kevin Costner walked with bow and arrows in hand through the set of his next film, *Robin Hood: Prince of Thieves*. Director and good friend Kevin Reynolds pointed at the weapon and asked, "Have you actually learned how to shoot that thing?" Costner off-handedly answered, "Yeah." To prove it, he turned, focused his clear gray-blue eyes and shot at a target 30 yards out. A direct hit! "It was amazing," stated Reynolds.

There's no doubt about it, Kevin Costner **is** amazing and his aim is right on target. Whether shooting an Old West six-gun or medieval English bow and arrow, Costner has hit the mark as Hollywood's hottest new leading man.

"I'm a run-and-jumper," says the ever-active Kevin Costner. Having just seen his movie *Dances With Wolves* sweep the 1990 Oscars with 12 nominations and seven awards (including Best Picture and Best Director), Costner is running and jumping down the road of success. However, as with most success stories, it was a rough road traveled by only his own determination and hard work.

BASEBALL, BUSINESS OR ACTING?

A California native, Kevin Costner was born January 18, 1955 in the Los Angeles suburb of Lynwood. His father worked for the Southern California Edison Company. As the elder Costner was promoted, the family moved to many different locations. Kevin frequently found himself transferred to a new school. Kevin's four years in high school were all at different schools, although he finally graduated from Villa Park High in Orange County.

Always the "new" kid, Costner was a thin, shy teen-ager. Describing himself as a "late bloomer," Costner stood nearly a foot shorter in high school than his current 6'1". However, his height never stopped him from becoming an avid sports buff and taking part in baseball, basketball, and football. "Athletics was a savior, 'cause you could immediately get a set of friends," says Costner.

At that time, he could think of nothing better than becoming a professional baseball player. After high school, however, Costner chose business over baseball. He went on to California State University in Fullerton, studying marketing and finance. However, behind the schoolwork, he discovered the South Coast Actors' Co-Op and began appearing in community theater productions. He wasn't sure where this was all leading, but as he states, "With acting, I was on fire."

In March 1975, Costner met "Snow White" at a college fraternity party. Cindy Silva, whose summer job at Disneyland was to play Snow White, soon decided she had found her "Prince Charming." After Costner graduated from college in 1978, they were married.

Costner found work with a marketing firm. After only 30 days, he told off the company's biggest account, went home and surprised Cindy with, "Well, I quit today. I'm going to become an actor and a writer." Thunderstruck, Cindy reminded him that he could barely spell.

With no special training, no agent, and no show-business connections, Costner began to plan his acting career. Commercials and bad "beach" films were his beginning. A perfectionist, he knew this wasn't right. "I wanted to do the best work with the best people," states Costner.

He didn't quit, but he took a step back and began studying acting and doing some community theater work. "I was horrible," says Costner. "I was as bad as you can be, but something about being horrible increased my desire for it." Through sheer determination, Costner started his movie career.

PLAYING DEAD: *THE BIG CHILL*

Costner's first big break seemed about to happen with the 1983 movie *The Big Chill*. Cast as a young man whose suicide brings together his college friends, Costner's character, Alex, was seen only in "flashbacks" — scenes where his friends remembered him. However, what he thought would be the start of something big ended up being edited from the movie altogether. Two

Kevin and Cindy Costner.

weeks before the film was to be released, director Larry Kasdan had the sad duty to call and inform Kevin that Costner's three months of work was now on the cutting-room floor. Costner's response, "I thought it might happen. Don't you think I'm taking this well?"

Even though he was laughingly known in the industry as the guy cut from *The Big Chill*, Costner determinedly refused to quit. During this time, Costner got a new role — that of a father. Cindy, who had long-since given up her Snow White job to work in the office of Delta Air Lines, gave birth to their first daughter, Annie.

Bit parts and theater work followed. Then in 1985 Costner found himself in three films: As "Jake," a western gunslinger in *Silverado*, as one of two brothers (one dying) who enter a bicycle marathon in *American Flyers*, and the leading roll in *Fandango*, where he played a fraternity wildman who leads his buddies on one last adventure in the desert. All three were less than successful at the box office.

Rather than accept work that he did not believe in or like, Costner passed on all scripts for the next year and a half. However, his chilling experiences were about to warm up significantly.

TOUCHING SUCCESS

By 1987, the Costners had another daughter, Lily, and Kevin found the script that he'd been waiting for. Cast as the heroic Chicago detective Eliot Ness in *The Untouchables*, the clean-cut Costner brought a new perspective to the role. Directed by Brian De Palma, Costner turned the previously-portrayed Ness character from rough and grim to tough and honest. States Costner, "Whomever I play, I enter his world." Costner makes his role believable by "trying to be as honorable to the character as you can."

Costner's straight acting clearly showed up on the screen. Plus, playing opposite the masterful talents of Robert De Niro as the infamous gangster Al Capone, and Sean Connery as a street-smart cop and Ness' right-hand man, Costner's name was suddenly linked with their success.

Costner as detective Eliot Ness in The Untouchables.

Andy Garcia, Sean Connery, Kevin Costner and Charles Martin Smith are Federal Treasury investigators fighting to stop ganster Al Capone in The Untouchables.

His straightforward, maintain-the-character style also showed through in the second film he starred in that year, *No Way Out*. Although not as successful as *The Untouchables*, Costner's portrayal of the secretive U.S. Navy Officer Tom Farrell had audiences believing the character's loyalty to America up to the end.

Sean Young with Kevin Costner as U.S. Navy Officer Tom Farrell in No Way Out.

FIELDING HIS DREAMS

Mixing business with pleasure, Costner's next roles allowed him to combine acting with his love of baseball. Against advice from people who feared Costner would stereotype himself into one type of role, Costner acted in two baseball pictures back-to-back.

First came the successful *Bull Durham* in 1988. Playing veteran catcher Crash Davis, Costner's role was to teach a young upstart pitcher, Nuke (played by Tim Robbins), the tricks of the game. The picture also starred Susan Sarandon as a woman in love with the game and the players. It received an Academy Award nomination for Best Original Screenplay and was well received by audiences across the country.

Kevin Costner portrays Ray Kinsella, an Iowa farmer who heeds a mysterious voice and builds a baseball diamond in Field of Dreams.

From the dusty playing field, Costner moved to the cornfields of Iowa in 1989. In *Field of Dreams*, he played Ray Kinsella, an Iowa farmer who hears a voice tell him: "If you build it, he will come." Based on the novel "Shoeless Joe," by W.P. Kinsella, the "it" turns out to be a baseball field. The "he" at first appears to be the ghost of legendary Shoeless Joe Jackson, the great left fielder who was suspended from baseball for his role in throwing the 1919 World Series. However, a trail of clues leads Kinsella on a round-about hunt with the help of James Earl Jones' character Terence Mann, and later discovers the "he" to be the spirit of Ray Kinsella's father.

Again, Costner's honest, straightforward approach made the Ray Kinsella character appealing and believable. At one point in the movie, a ghostly ballplayer asks, "Is this heaven?" Costner's character answers, "No, it's Iowa." But with its success, including an Academy Award nomination for Best Picture, as well as the birth of his son Joe, Costner himself felt like he really was in heaven.

Yet, Hollywood is always up and down. Costner's next work, *Revenge*, was anything but heaven. Costner went into the picture knowing that the "script needed work." It did. Reviews were awful. People stayed away in droves. "What a miserable time," says Costner. "Talk about sticking your head up over a log in open hunting season."

It was time to try something else.

Field of Dreams, *with a nomination for Best Picture, was a dream come true for its star Kevin Costner.*

DIRECTING "*DANCES*"

What would be next for the man who likes to do things his way? First, he started his own production company. Tig Productions, named after his grandmother's nickname "Tig"— which is an Oklahoma word for wearing one's hair in rattails as she did—started operations with Costner's older brother, Dan, handling the finances.

Next, Costner decided to direct his first film and act in the starring role was well! Kevin Costner, not one to start small, jumped in with both feet. Taking friend Michael Blake's novel, Costner declared it "the clearest idea for a movie I'd ever read." The screenplay was written and became the $18 million, three-hour Western epic *Dances With Wolves*.

Costner, whose grandfather was half Cherokee Indian, insisted on the utmost accuracy in the picture. "I felt that economically, it was too big a risk to make a movie about Indians and not treat them right...It's just easier to go with the truth." The "truth" meant filming the picture in Lakota Sioux tongue with subtitles. The "truth" meant location work on the South Dakota plains — 115° F blazing heat in the summer and 20° F freezing cold in the fall. And the "truth" meant taking the time to tell the whole story — three hours, not cut to Hollywood's standard of two hours. "Somebody else might not have done subtitles. I wanted to see it in the Native American lan-

Lt. John Dunbar (Kevin Costner) rides out on Cisco.

guage. Somebody else might have made it shorter, because they don't think people can sit with this movie. I think they can," states Costner.

The film centered on U.S. Cavalry Lieutenant John Dunbar, a Union soldier in 1864. A suicide ride across enemy lines elevates him to the rank of hero and earns him a military reward. Dunbar is allowed to choose where he wishes to be stationed and is given Cisco, the horse that carried him on his wild ride. Dunbar goes west to single-handedly man the furthest military outpost. At first, his only companions are Cisco and a wolf with two white feet he names Two Socks. Soon, however, Dunbar meets his neighbors: the Lakota Sioux.

Costner dressed as his character Lt. Dunbar directs Dances with Wolves.

Befriended by a holy man, Kicking Bird (played by Graham Greene an Oneida Indian from Canada), Dunbar slowly wins the Indians' trust and learns their ways.

He is first called "Loo Ten Tant," but one day, while riding over to their camp, Two Socks follows him. He gets off his horse and tries to shoo the wolf away. The Indians watch his strange antics and a new name is given him: "Dances With Wolves." Eventually, he joins their tribe, marrying a captured white woman known as Stands With a Fist (played by Mary McDonnell).

Using Native American tongue in the picture meant immense work for some of the actors. While Costner's character slowly learns the language through the picture, other characters, such as Greene's Kicking Bird, McDonnell's Stands With a Fist, and the wild untrusting character of Wind in His Hair (played by Rodney Grant, an Omaha Indian from the banks of the Missouri River) had to be fluent, which meant hours and hours of language instruction.

To accurately depict Lt. Dunbar on screen, Costner also insisted on doing many of his own stunts. His reputation for taking chances had already made him an insurance risk. In *Silverado*, he rode bareback. *Bull Durham* showed Costner doing all his own throwing, catching and sliding. In *No Way Out*, Costner ran into a moving car and tumbled across its hood. On a windy day in Chicago, the set of *The Untouchables* found Costner racing along the edge of a rooftop 120 feet above the ground. He could do no less in his own picture.

During a buffalo hunt, Costner's character rides with his Native American friends into a sea of 3,500 buffaloes. An accidental crash between himself and another rider flung the director/star off his horse. Twisting in mid-air, Costner dropped backwards onto the dirt. As screenwriter, Michael Blake described it, "Kevin hit the ground, bounced about two feet straight up in the air and rolled over like a big sack of flour." Costner's stunt double, Norman Howell, immediately raced to his side. Shaken and a little dazed, Costner got up, dusted off and stated, "I want to ride."

Orion Pictures, the company that agreed to finance and distribute the film, naturally worried about their star and their investment. "I'm not doing things I don't think I can do," stated Costner. Two other falls brought him down, but as always, he got back on his horse and kept going.

Costner wanted the film done his way, and so it was. "I ended up doing everything I wanted." The outcome? A sweeping box-office success that met with approval not only from critics and the general public, but by Native Americans as well. In fact, so pleased with the depiction and loyalty to the story, the Sioux nation adopted Costner as a member of its tribal family on October 19, 1990.

John Dunbar (Kevin Costner) and Stands With A Fist (Mary McDonnell) take a romantic walk in the woods.

"I knew I was going to experiment," says Costner. His experiment paid off in a $5 million take-home pay for himself, as well as a sweep of the 63rd Annual Academy Awards including: Best Picture, Best Director, Best Adapted Screenplay, Best Cinematography, Best Film Editing, Best Music Original Score, and Best Sound.

As Costner states, "People don't go into directing for power. They go in for the completion of something they want to see." Costner saw his dream realized.

Kevin Costner holds up the Oscars for Best Director and Best Picture for his film Dances With Wolves.

TROUBLESHOOTING IN ENGLAND

Three days after completing *"Dances,"* Costner moved from the Old West to Merry Olde England and onto the London set of *Robin Hood: Prince of Thieves*. Kevin Reynolds, who had directed the 1985 *Fandango*, was chosen by Morgan Creek Productions to direct the $50 million action-adventure feature. Costner was looking forward to working with his friend again. However, the ups and downs of Hollywood once again followed him across the sea.

Two other production companies were believed to be producing *"Robin Hood"* films, and suddenly it became vitally necessary to be the first one done and in theaters. (It was later learned that one production was stopped and the other became a TV movie.) This meant trying to beat the English winter and shortening the shooting schedule from 15 to 13 weeks. That meant going without rehearsals and working 12 hours a day and six days a week. It meant Costner had to learn his lines and a good English accent right away. It meant they had to fill the roles of Maid Marian and the Sheriff of Nottingham immediately. Mary Elizabeth Mastrantonio and Alan Rickman were quickly chosen to successfully complete the casting.

As with anything rushed, tensions were high. What both Costner and Reynolds had hoped would be a fun adven-

Kevin Costner in Robin Hood: Prince of Thieves.

ture turned into a nightmare of work and frustration. Costner found he couldn't concentrate on his English accent and do his best acting. Finally, Reynolds instructed him to concentrate on the acting. (They went back later to redo the lines with the appropriate accent.)

Costner, once again, brought up his insurance rates with risky stunts he had to do. The first came at the beginning of the picture. In the story, Robin arrives back on English shores with his Moorish companion Azeem (played by Morgan Freeman) after being gone for five years fighting in the Crusades. Costner's part was to jump out of a longboat and kiss the ground. Gale warnings were issued on the day of the shoot. The owners wouldn't let the longboat out on the water, so a smaller rowboat was found.

States Costner, "It was probably the most dangerous thing I've ever done in the movies, and it would never look like it, because I'm sitting in a boat. But I have these clothes on that if I'd fallen overboard—it was a really low boat—I would have drowned. I would have gone right to the bottom, there's no doubt in my mind." The scene was shot over and over, until finally Costner was so cold and tired he was unable to lift himself out of the boat. It was a bad start to a bad shoot. And what's worse, after all that work, neither Reynolds nor Costner liked what they saw—the boat was just too small. Weeks later, at the end of the shooting, the whole scene was done over with a longboat.

This was not the only work in the water, nor the only dangers Costner took. He also learned swordplay and quarterstaff fighting. In the scene where Robin Hood first meets the character John Little, more popularly known as "Little John" (played by Nick Brimble), Robin and Little John take their quarterstaffs (seven-foot-long, three-and-a-half-inch thick wooden poles) and battle it out at Aysgarth Falls. From morning until night for four full days, the two took turns knocking each other into the freezing waters. Brimble states, "I remember on the first day, I wasn't too eager to get whacked about the head myself, but I was even more nervous about whacking out our star. And Kevin Costner said, 'Really *hit* me.' And I had to really hit him... And the extraordinary thing about Costner is he seems to *like* all that."

As with any production, there were some good-humored teasing on the set. Since the 1920s, at least twenty "*Robin Hood*" productions have been produced—everything from early black-and-white films to a Walt Disney animated picture. In most productions, Robin Hood is dressed in green tights and a green hat with a feather. Costume designer John Bloomfield had come up with a more "manly" outfit for Costner, which included rough-textured, studded leather. However, Bloomfield couldn't resist playing a practical joke on Costner and laid out the tradition Robin Hood-ware. Needless to say, Costner walked in and looked in shock at the fake outfit. "They let me think that was my costume—but not for long," laughs Costner.

Although the production was tiring and both Costner and director Reynolds were worried that the rushed schedule would make for a less-than-perfect movie, *Robin Hood: Prince of Thieves* opened mid-June 1991 with the second-largest box-office opening weekend for a non-sequel movie (first largest was the 1990 film *Batman*). Even with all the trouble, Costner again brought success to the screen.

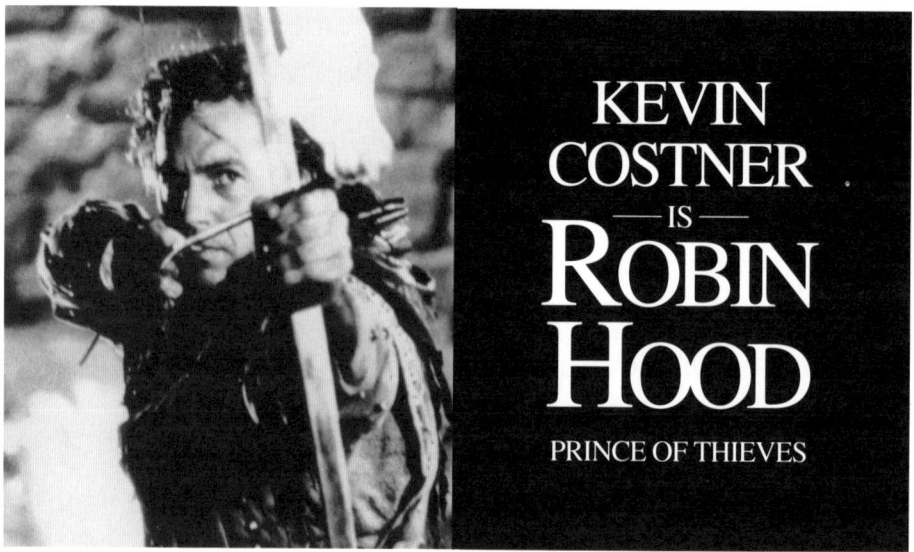

STAR STATUS

Although truly a star, Kevin Costner maintains an honest, down-to-earth attitude, enjoying his fame but not being swept away by it. Says Costner, "I don't say something I can't back up. I don't make a promise I can't keep." It's this honesty and hard work that have brought him star status, and he's not abandoning these qualities now that he's reached the top. Nor has he forgotten the fans who have helped him get to the top.

Sean Dunlap, a 14-year-old boy with muscle cancer, wanted to see *Robin Hood*, but he was weakening and it was clear that he wouldn't live until the mid-June 1991 opening. When Costner learned of the teen-ager's situation, the actor arranged a private preview of the movie for Sean and some family and friends. On June 1st, Sean enjoyed the action-adventure film sitting right next to its star, Costner himself. A week later, the young man passed away.

Flying high on the wings of success, Kevin Costner is continuing to learn and build on his acting/directing career. Already, the 36-year-old star is hard at work on his next acting project. Costner plays New Orleans district attorney, Jim Garrison in Warner Brothers' production of *JFK*, the story of the assassination of President John F. Kennedy.

"I know even today that I'm not as good as I'm going to be," says Costner. "But I have a right to get better." Movie-goers across the country can only look forward to tomorrow, and prepare to enjoy the ever-growing talents of Kevin Costner.

Kevin Costner and his wife Cindy attend the 63rd Academy Awards.

Kevin Costner: award-winning actor/director.

KEVIN COSTNER'S ADDRESS

You may write to Kevin Costner at:

Kevin Costner
c/o Creative Artists Agency, Inc.
9830 Wilshire Boulevard
Beverly Hills, CA 90212-1825

Juan Gonzalez

HISPANICS OF ACHIEVEMENT

CONSULTING EDITORS

RODOLFO CARDONA
*professor of Spanish and comparative literature,
Boston University*

JAMES COCKCROFT
*visiting professor of Latin American and Caribbean studies,
State University of New York at Albany*

HISPANICS OF ACHIEVEMENT

Juan Gonzalez

Dennis R. Tuttle

CHELSEA HOUSE PUBLISHERS
NEW YORK ■ PHILADELPHIA

To the children of Latin America, many of whom use a fig leaf, bottle cap, and tobacco stick as a baseball glove, ball, and bat.

The author wishes to acknowledge his gratitude to the many coaches and players whose openness and participation contributed greatly to this project. But there are also a number of others, not mentioned in the book, whose professionalism, advice, legwork, and expertise proved invaluable: Fernando Cuza, Ramon Maldonado, T. R. Sullivan, Joe Szadkowski, Stacy Travers, and Lonnie Wheeler. Special thanks are due to Luis Mayoral, whose guidance, friendship, perception, and tolerance made this book eminently possible.

CHELSEA HOUSE PUBLISHERS

Editorial Director: Richard Rennert
Executive Managing Editor: Karyn Gullen Browne
Copy Chief: Robin James
Picture Editor: Adrian G. Allen
Creative Director: Robert Mitchell
Art Director: Joan Ferrigno
Production Manager: Sallye Scott

HISPANICS OF ACHIEVEMENT
Senior Editor: Philip Koslow

Staff for *JUAN GONZALEZ*
Editorial Assistant: Annie McDonnell
Designer: M. Cambraia Magalhães
Picture Researcher: Villette Harris
Cover Illustrator: Daniel O'Leary

Copyright © 1995 by Chelsea House Publishers, a division of Main Line Book Co. All rights reserved. Printed and bound in the United States of America.

First Printing
1 3 5 7 9 8 6 4 2

Library of Congress Cataloging-in-Publication Data
Tuttle, Dennis R.
Juan Gonzalez/Dennis R. Tuttle
p. cm.—(Hispanics of achievement)
Includes bibliographical references and index.
ISBN 0-7910-1948-9
ISBN 0-7910-1949-7 (pbk.)
1. Gonzalez, Juan, 1969– —Juvenile literature. 2. Baseball players—Puerto Rico—Biography—Juvenile literature. [1. Gonzalez, Juan, 1969– . 2. Baseball players. 3. Puerto Ricans—Biography.] I. Title. II. Series.
94-42469
GV865.A1G6657 1995
CIP
796.357'092—dc20
AC
[B]

CONTENTS

Hispanics of Achievement	7
A New Superstar	15
Twenty Years Between Heroes	23
Something Special	39
New Culture, New Language	49
Igor the Magnificent	59
Home Run King	69
"He Is a Friend to All"	85
Destined for Cooperstown?	95
Appendix: Comparative Statistics	104
Chronology	105
Further Reading	107
Index	109

HISPANICS OF ACHIEVEMENT

JOAN BAEZ
Mexican-American folksinger

RUBÉN BLADES
Panamanian lawyer and entertainer

JORGE LUIS BORGES
Argentine writer

PABLO CASALS
Spanish cellist and conductor

MIGUEL DE CERVANTES
Spanish writer

CESAR CHAVEZ
Mexican-American labor leader

JULIO CÉSAR CHÁVEZ
Mexican boxing champion

EL CID
Spanish military leader

HENRY CISNEROS
Mexican-American political leader

ROBERTO CLEMENTE
Puerto Rican baseball player

SALVADOR DALÍ
Spanish painter

PLÁCIDO DOMINGO
Spanish singer

GLORIA ESTEFAN
Cuban-American singer

GABRIEL GARCÍA MÁRQUEZ
Colombian writer

FRANCISCO JOSÉ DE GOYA
Spanish painter

JULIO IGLESIAS
Spanish singer

RAUL JULIA
Puerto Rican actor

FRIDA KAHLO
Mexican painter

JOSÉ MARTÍ
Cuban revolutionary and poet

RITA MORENO
Puerto Rican singer and actress

PABLO NERUDA
Chilean poet and diplomat

OCTAVIO PAZ
Mexican poet and critic

PABLO PICASSO
Spanish artist

ANTHONY QUINN
Mexican-American actor

DIEGO RIVERA
Mexican painter

LINDA RONSTADT
Mexican-American singer

ANTONIO LÓPEZ DE SANTA ANNA
Mexican general and politician

GEORGE SANTAYANA
Spanish philosopher and poet

JUNÍPERO SERRA
Spanish missionary and explorer

LEE TREVINO
Mexican-American golfer

PANCHO VILLA
Mexican revolutionary

CHELSEA HOUSE PUBLISHERS

INTRODUCTION

HISPANICS OF ACHIEVEMENT

Rodolfo Cardona

The Spanish language and many other elements of Spanish culture are present in the United States today and have been since the country's earliest beginnings. Some of these elements have come directly from the Iberian Peninsula; others have come indirectly, by way of Mexico, the Caribbean basin, and the countries of Central and South America.

Spanish culture has influenced America in many subtle ways, and consequently many Americans remain relatively unaware of the extent of its impact. The vast majority of them recognize the influence of Spanish culture in America, but they often do not realize the great importance and long history of that influence. This is partly because Americans have tended to judge the Hispanic influence in the United States in statistical terms rather than to look closely at the ways in which individual Hispanics have profoundly affected American culture. For this reason, it is fitting that Americans obtain more than a passing acquaintance with the origins of these Spanish cultural elements and gain an understanding of how they have been woven into the fabric of American society.

It is well documented that Spanish seafarers were the first to explore and colonize many of the early territories of what is today called the United States of America. For this reason, students of geography discover Hispanic names all over the map of the United States. For instance, the Strait of Juan de Fuca was named after the Spanish explorer who first navigated the waters of the Pacific Northwest; the names of states such as Arizona (arid zone), Montana (mountain), Florida (thus named because it was reached on Easter Sunday, which in Spanish is called the feast of Pascua Florida), and California (named after a fictitious land in one of the first and probably the most popular among the Spanish novels of chivalry, *Amadis of Gaul*) are all derived from Spanish; and there are numerous mountains, rivers, canyons, towns, and cities with Spanish names throughout the United States.

Not only explorers but many other illustrious figures in Spanish history have helped define American culture. For example, the 13th-century king of Spain, Alfonso X, also known as the Learned, may be unknown to the majority of Americans, but his work on the codification of Spanish law has greatly influenced the evolution of American law, particularly in the jurisdictions of the Southwest. For this contribution a statue of him stands in the rotunda of the Capitol in Washington, D.C. Likewise, the name Diego Rivera may be unfamiliar to most Americans, but this Mexican painter influenced many American artists whose paintings, commissioned during the Great Depression and the New Deal era of the 1930s, adorn the walls of government buildings throughout the United States. In recent years the contributions of Puerto Ricans, Mexicans, Mexican Americans (Chicanos), and Cubans in American cities such as Boston, Chicago, Los Angeles, Miami, Minneapolis, New York, and San Antonio have been enormous.

The importance of the Spanish language in this vast cultural complex cannot be overstated. Spanish, after all, is second only to English as the most widely spoken of Western languages within the United States as well as in the entire world. The popularity of the Spanish language in America has a long history.

In addition to Spanish exploration of the New World, the great Spanish literary tradition served as a vehicle for bringing the language and culture to America. Interest in Spanish literature in America began when English immigrants brought with them translations of Spanish masterpieces of the Golden Age. As early as 1683, private libraries in Philadelphia and Boston contained copies of the first picaresque novel, *Lazarillo de Tormes*, translations of Francisco de Quevedo's *Los Sueños*, and copies of the immortal epic of reality and illusion *Don Quixote*, by the great Spanish writer Miguel de Cervantes. It would not be surprising if Cotton Mather, the arch-Puritan, read *Don Quixote* in its original Spanish, if only to enrich his vocabulary in preparation for his writing *La fe del cristiano en 24 artículos de la Institución de Cristo, enviada a los españoles para que abran sus ojos* (The Christian's Faith in 24 Articles of the Institution of Christ, Sent to the Spaniards to Open Their Eyes), published in Boston in 1699.

Over the years, Spanish authors and their works have had a vast influence on American literature—from Washington Irving, John Steinbeck, and Ernest Hemingway in the novel to Henry Wadsworth Longfellow and Archibald MacLeish in poetry. Such important American writers as James Fenimore Cooper, Edgar Allan Poe, Walt Whitman, Mark Twain, and Herman Melville all owe a sizable debt to the Spanish literary tradition. Some writers, such as Willa Cather and Maxwell Anderson, who explored Spanish themes they came into contact with in the American Southwest and Mexico, were influenced less directly but no less profoundly.

Important contributions to a knowledge of Spanish culture in the United States were also made by many lesser known individuals—teachers, publishers, historians, entrepreneurs, and others—with a love for Spanish culture. One of the most significant of these contributions was made by Abiel Smith, a Harvard College graduate of the class of 1764, when he bequeathed stock worth $20,000 to Harvard for the support of a professor of French and Spanish. By 1819 this endowment had produced enough income to appoint a professor, and the philologist and humanist George Ticknor became the first holder of the Abiel

Smith Chair, which was the very first endowed Chair at Harvard University. Other illustrious holders of the Smith Chair would include the poets Henry Wadsworth Longfellow and James Russell Lowell.

A highly respected teacher and scholar, Ticknor was also a collector of Spanish books, and as such he made a very special contribution to America's knowledge of Spanish culture. He was instrumental in amassing for Harvard libraries one of the first and most impressive collections of Spanish books in the United States. He also had a valuable personal collection of Spanish books and manuscripts, which he bequeathed to the Boston Public Library.

With the creation of the Abiel Smith Chair, Spanish language and literature courses became part of the curriculum at Harvard, which also went on to become the first American university to offer graduate studies in Romance languages. Other colleges and universities throughout the United States gradually followed Harvard's example, and today Spanish language and culture may be studied at most American institutions of higher learning.

No discussion of the Spanish influence in the United States, however brief, would be complete without a mention of the Spanish influence on art. Important American artists such as John Singer Sargent, James A. M. Whistler, Thomas Eakins, and Mary Cassatt all explored Spanish subjects and experimented with Spanish techniques. Virtually every serious American artist living today has studied the work of the Spanish masters as well as the great 20th-century Spanish painters Salvador Dalí, Joan Miró, and Pablo Picasso.

The most pervasive Spanish influence in America, however, has probably been in music. Compositions such as Leonard Bernstein's *West Side Story*, the Latinization of William Shakespeare's *Romeo and Juliet* set in New York's Puerto Rican quarter, and Aaron Copland's *Salon Mexico* are two obvious examples. In general, one can hear the influence of Latin rhythms—from tango to mambo, from guaracha to salsa—in virtually every form of American music.

INTRODUCTION

This series of biographies, which Chelsea House has published under the general title HISPANICS OF ACHIEVEMENT, constitutes further recognition of—and a renewed effort to bring forth to the consciousness of America's young people—the contributions that Hispanic people have made not only in the United States but throughout the civilized world. The men and women who are featured in this series have attained a high level of accomplishment in their respective fields of endeavor and have made a permanent mark on American society.

The title of this series must be understood in its broadest possible sense: The term *Hispanics* is intended to include Spaniards, Spanish Americans, and individuals from many countries whose language and culture have either direct or indirect Spanish origins. The names of many of the people included in this series will be immediately familiar; others will be less recognizable. All, however, have attained recognition within their own countries, and often their fame has transcended their borders.

The series HISPANICS OF ACHIEVEMENT thus addresses the attainments and struggles of Hispanic people in the United States and seeks to tell the stories of individuals whose personal and professional lives in some way reflect the larger Hispanic experience. These stories are exemplary of what human beings can accomplish, often against daunting odds and by extraordinary personal sacrifice, where there is conviction and determination. Fray Junípero Serra, the 18th-century Spanish Franciscan missionary, is one such individual. Although in very poor health, he devoted the last 15 years of his life to the foundation of missions throughout California—then a mostly unsettled expanse of land—in an effort to bring a better life to Native Americans through the cultivation of crafts and animal husbandry. An example from recent times, the Mexican-American labor leader Cesar Chavez battled bitter opposition and made untold personal sacrifices in his effort to help poor agricultural workers who have been exploited for decades on farms throughout the Southwest.

The talent with which each one of these men and women may have been endowed required dedication and hard work to develop and become fully realized. Many of them have enjoyed rewards for their efforts during their own lifetime, whereas others have died poor and unrecognized. For some it took a long time to achieve their goals, for others success came at an early age, and for still others the struggle continues. All of them, however, stand out as people whose lives have made a difference, whose achievements we need to recognize today and should continue to honor in the future.

Juan Gonzalez

NATIONAL
JUSTICE 02
PIAZZA 00
HOME RUN
JUAN GONZALEZ
AMERICAN 21
SONY
HIT IT

CHAPTER ONE

A NEW SUPERSTAR

The baseball kept rising and rising into the Baltimore backdrop, cutting through the summer humidity like a rocket sled on rails. When the ball suddenly stopped and fell into the stunned crowd below, it was only because the upper deck of Oriole Park at Camden Yards had gotten in its way.

The 47,981 fans watching the 1993 All-Star Game home run–hitting contest stood and gazed at the distance the ball had traveled, marveling at the speed with which it had left the playing field. The blast was measured at 473 feet from home plate. Since no player had come close to hitting a ball that far at Camden Yards, the crowd did not know whether to cheer wildly or go into shock. Most of the spectators, like the All-Star players and coaches watching from the dugouts, simply pointed in disbelief at the spot the baseball had hit.

"He definitely had a stewardess on that ball," said an awestruck Ken Griffey, Jr., of the Seattle Mariners, himself one of the game's premier long-ball hitters.

With one swing of his long black Cooper bat, Juan Gonzalez of the Texas Rangers ceased to be the best-kept secret in major league baseball. The talent that fans and followers in Gonzalez's homeland of Puerto Rico had admired for almost three years was suddenly and impressively launched on the American public. With more than 600 reporters covering the home run–hitting contest and ESPN televising the event nationwide, the man affectionately called "Igor" by

Juan Gonzalez hoists his trophy after winning the home run–hitting contest prior to the 1993 All-Star Game.

15

his friends and family sent a wake-up call by outslugging Griffey in the most eye-popping performance of his young career.

With his muscular arms and powerful right-handed swing, Gonzalez hit 12 home runs in just 27 at-bats that day. Oddly, even though he had been the 1992 major league home run champion with 43, he was not even the favorite going into the contest. Griffey, Cecil Fielder of the Detroit Tigers, Barry Bonds of the San Francisco Giants, and David Justice of the Atlanta Braves were better-known home run hitters. But Gonzalez wasted little time placing his name among the game's best.

He promptly hit seven homers in 17 swings and tied Griffey for the contest lead. Since no prior All-Star home run contest had ended in a tie, officials debated whether to make Griffey and Gonzalez co-champions or have a playoff. Since it was a beautiful, sun-splashed day and the crowd was already excited, everyone agreed it would be more fun to just let Griffey and Gonzalez slug it out.

The rules were simple: each ball not hit out of the park served as an out. During the regular contest, each player got 10 outs. For the playoff, only 5 outs were allowed. The crowd stood with anticipation of each blast.

The left-hand-hitting Griffey had brought the fans to their feet earlier in the contest, when he became the first player to hit the old B&O warehouse beyond the right-field wall, belting a high drive of 445 feet. He failed to hit the warehouse again in the playoff, but he did manage four homers in nine swings.

In the playoff, Gonzalez bettered Griffey's warehouse homer with his now-famous upper deck shot. But he was not finished. He drove another shot off the ivy-covered wall way beyond the center-field fence,

A NEW SUPERSTAR

455 feet from the plate. Another landed in the back bullpen in left-center field. Those three home runs traveled a combined 1,223 feet. "I didn't hear any sirens," pondered Baltimore Orioles manager Johnny Oates. "Did anybody get hurt on those things?"

Gonzalez finished with five homers, one more than Griffey, to win the playoff. His peers and the press were astonished by the pure strength and distance of his blasts. "Griffey hit the warehouse, but the power is here," Gonzalez said, smiling ear to ear while tapping the barrel of the bat against the palm of his hand.

Gonzalez's performance led to great anticipation for the All-Star Game itself. He was batting .320 with 23 homers and 60 RBI at the break. Yet, he had placed only seventh in the fans' voting for outfielders, finishing well behind starters Griffey, Kirby Puckett of the Minnesota Twins, and Joe Carter of the Toronto

Gonzalez launches one of his 12 home runs during the July 12 contest held at Baltimore's Camden Yards. Though he had led the American League in home runs the previous year, Gonzalez achieved national celebrity only after winning the All-Star contest.

Blue Jays. Gonzalez had received 899,539 votes, but Griffey, the top vote getter, had garnered 2.69 million. Gonzalez was selected to the team by Toronto manager Cito Gaston, who had overlooked him for the 1992 All-Star Game despite the fact that Gonzalez was leading the league in home runs at the time.

As it turned out, Gonzalez's moment of fame—and the turning point of his career—was the home run–hitting contest rather than the game itself. With the crowd anxious for a repeat of his contest performance, Gonzalez struck out and walked in his two at-bats. But he was cheered enthusiastically before and after each turn at the plate.

Gonzalez became an instant star. Though previously he had been hampered by a language barrier with fans and reporters, his home runs spoke a universal language. His batting practices started drawing huge and enthusiastic crowds in each city the Rangers visited. His home run–hitting power brought media attention unlike any he had experienced. Television, magazines, and newspapers all wanted to know more about him. Shy and private, Gonzalez could no longer play in the shadow of his teammate, the legendary Nolan Ryan. "The home run hitting contest at the All-Star Game elevated him one more rung up the ladder as far as celebrity status," Rangers general manager Tom Grieve told *USA Today Baseball Weekly*.

Suddenly, Gonzalez found himself swamped with requests for interviews and appearances. The pressure also mounted for him to perform as the Rangers remained in the pennant race. They eventually finished second to Chicago in the American League West Division. Mildly distracted but not overwhelmed by the sudden swarm of attention, Gonzalez hit 20 homers over July and August to help him finish with 46 for the year and win the American League home run title again. As a result, Gonzalez became the first American

Seattle Mariners slugger Ken Griffey, Jr., shown here with his father, a former standout with the Cincinnati Reds and New York Yankees. During the 1993 home run contest, Griffey and Gonzalez put on a spectacular show of long-ball hitting, with the Texas star edging out his rival by one home run.

Leaguer in 15 years to win back-to-back home run titles. And he was only 23 years old when the season ended.

"I always knew, I always had this feeling, that something big was going to happen to me," Gonzalez said in a *Sports Illustrated* interview. "God gives me certain flashes. It's hard to describe. It's something natural. It's like a joy that I feel."

Over the first three seasons of his big league career, Gonzalez had quietly been the best home run hitter in baseball. He averaged a home run every 15 at-bats, and he hit a major league–leading 89 homers over the 1992 and 1993 seasons. But because of his limited command of English and Nolan Ryan's popularity with the reporters and fans at the close of his great career, Gonzalez was able to sit in his own corner of the clubhouse without much attention. In one regard, he liked it that way. The situation changed quickly after July 12, 1993.

"Interest had started, like in spring training. But it reached a peak after the home run championship in Baltimore," said the Rangers' assistant director of public relations, Luis Mayoral, a Spanish broadcaster and brother figure who helped Gonzalez and other Spanish-speaking players communicate with the American media and public. "People began to get interested in him not just for his raw power, but for what he's all about. It put him on center stage. The All-Star Game goes [on TV] all over the world. It goes to Latin America, Japan and Europe. From Anaheim to Seattle, Chicago, New York, it was really a launching pad for him."

It appeared the media and fans could not get enough of Juan Gonzalez, home run hitter. *USA Today* and *Baseball Weekly* did long feature stories on the rising star. The *Washington Post* profiled him not in the sports section but in the features. A Spanish-speaking writer from the *Times* of London did an interview by telephone while the Rangers were in Cleveland. A Japanese magazine featured him in a pictorial.

During the off-season the attention increased. *Life* magazine sent a reporter to Puerto Rico for a profile. The Dallas *Morning News* spent a week at Gonzalez's home. *Sports Illustrated for Kids* did a cover story, and *Tuff Stuff,* a sports collector's magazine, featured Gonzalez in its 1994 baseball issues.

While U.S. fans and reporters had been slow to recognize Gonzalez and his ability, fans in his homeland of Puerto Rico had made him a hero long before the 1993 All-Star Game. On an island where unemployment is widespread, poverty is common, and drugs are part of everyday life, Gonzalez had been a favorite since his rookie season of 1991. That year he hit 27 home runs and had 102 runs batted in. For the first time since the days of Orlando Cepeda, Tony Perez, Juan Marichal, and Roberto Clemente in the 1960s and early 1970s, Latin Americans had a new "patron saint," as *Sports Illustrated* called Gonzalez.

"We've had good players in Latin America throughout the years," Mayoral said. "But we have never really had a home run hitter since the days of Cepeda and Perez. There is always magic around a home run hitter."

To Latin Americans, Gonzalez's accomplishments in baseball were also their accomplishments. "He is a kid who is very smart, very sharp," observed Orlando Cepeda, who starred in the major leagues for 17 seasons. "He is very concerned about his people and concerned about his community, and he works very hard. He is very level-headed. He knows what he wants and what he needs to do for his community, his country. His popularity in Puerto Rico is huge. He is a god in Puerto Rico."

"We're a motivation and inspiration to so many young ones back home," Gonzalez added. "They can see there are other ways to live than to get lost in drugs and other negatives in life. I have to do my best to prove to the youth that hard work can accomplish anything."

Like his fans, Gonzalez often expected too much of himself. At times, he fell into the trap of trying to hit every ball out of the park, swinging too hard for the fences when a single to center field would have been just as good. He would get angry at himself for not helping his team in every at-bat, although the very nature of baseball requires players to accept failure as a part of the game. Once a player realizes that even the greatest hitters make outs approximately 70 percent of the time, the game is placed into focus and the pressure begins to lift. But in the case of a player like Gonzalez, the pressure was often stirred by the high expectations of others.

"In three or four years, every team in every league will have their core of hardcore fans that know the park, know the players, who will be able to point exactly to where Juan Gonzalez hit a ball," Tom Grieve said during that summer of 1993. "There's other great players who can hit the ball a long way—there's nobody who can hit them like Juan."

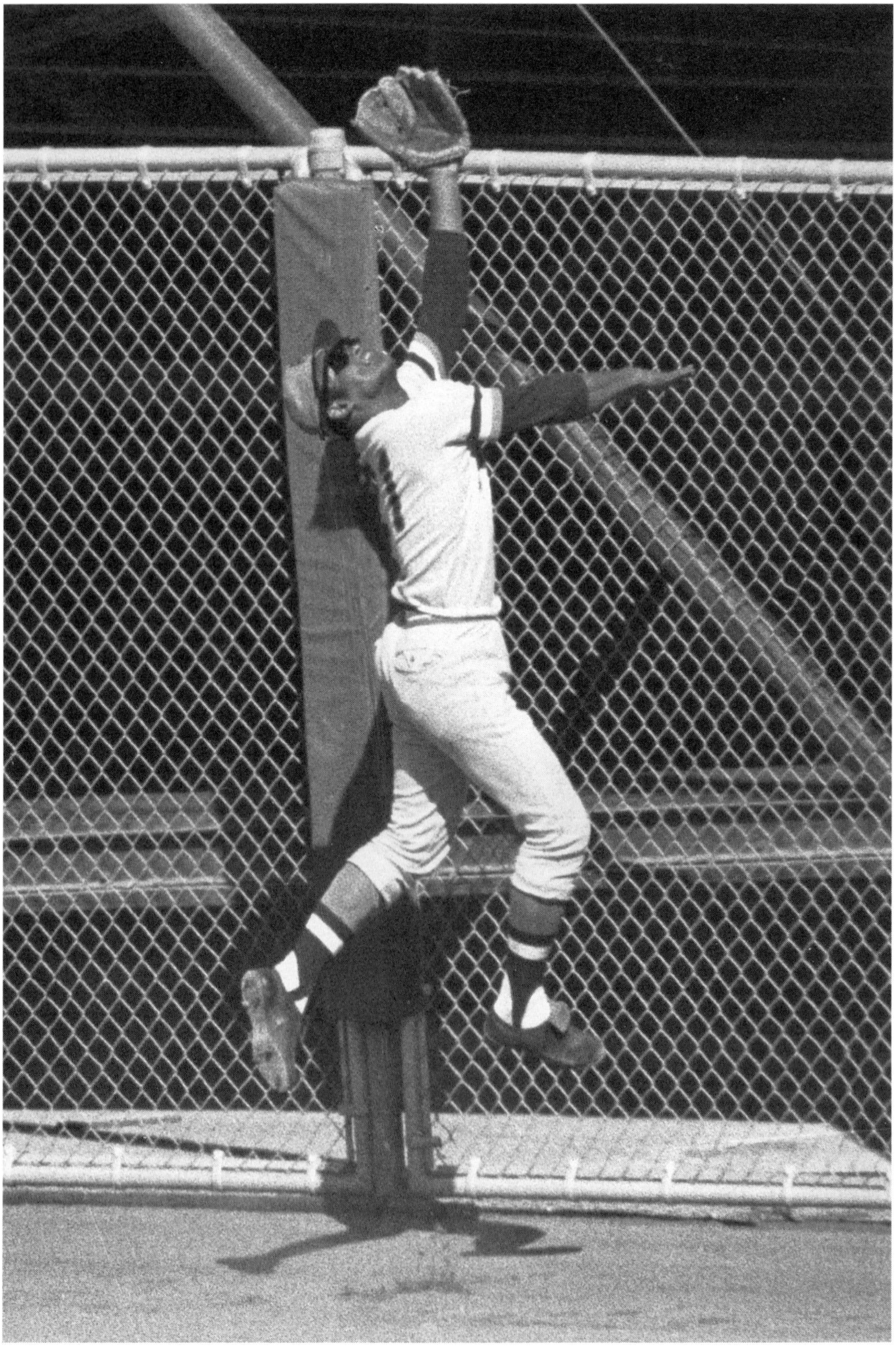

CHAPTER TWO

TWENTY YEARS BETWEEN HEROES

When Juan Gonzalez hit his 43rd homer on the last day of the 1992 season, he became the first Puerto Rican to win a home run championship since Orlando Cepeda led the National League with 46 in 1961, when he played for the San Francisco Giants. Gonzalez was only 22 years old, and he did not immediately appreciate the significance of his accomplishment. He was tired after the long season, and all his energies were focused on getting home to Puerto Rico.

When he arrived at the San Juan airport less than 30 hours after winning the crown, over 5,000 people met him with screams of "Igor, Igor!" Fifteen police motorcycles formed an escort for the 23-mile ride to Gonzalez's hometown of Vega Baja. Along the route, more than 100,000 people lined the expressway to see their new hero. Three thousand cheering fans awaited Gonzalez in Vega Baja's central plaza.

"How big is Juan here?" asked Pat Kelly, a winter league manager in Puerto Rico. "My players want baseballs to get him to autograph. He's like a god down here."

With a tinge of sadness, Gonzalez understands and accepts the Puerto Ricans' admiration. Since the great Hall of Famer Roberto Clemente died in a plane crash on New Year's Eve, 1972, Puerto Rico has been

Roberto Clemente (1934–72), one of baseball's all-time greats, attempts a spectacular leaping catch during a 1971 playoff contest. Clemente, who broke in with the Pittsburgh Pirates in 1955, was the first Puerto Rican ballplayer to achieve stardom in the major leagues.

without a sports hero to call its own. Many excellent Puerto Rican ballplayers have made the big leagues since Clemente's death, including a crop of young stars in the 1990s such as Carlos Baerga, Ivan Rodriguez, Ruben Sierra, and the Alomar brothers, Roberto and Sandy. But until Gonzalez and Baerga stepped forward, there had not been a player to bridge the gap of social needs in Puerto Rico and major league superstardom in the United States. "I can't be like Clemente on the playing field," Gonzalez once said. "That is another story. I do want to be like Clemente in caring."

Clemente, the most gifted and idolized Puerto Rican athlete ever, died a hero. He was riding in a small, overloaded airplane carrying food and clothes destined for Nicaragua, where an earthquake had devastated the city of Managua. The plane barely made it off the ground before crashing into the sea off San Juan. Clemente and the crew were killed, sending Puerto Rico into a state of shock and sadness.

Juan was only three years old at the time, so his knowledge of Clemente's good deeds comes secondhand. He has heard many stories from former ballplayers such as Orlando Cepeda and broadcasters such as Luis Mayoral. Each has told of Clemente's love for children, his generosity toward the needy, and his belief that if one man can help another, it is his divine responsibility to do so. "I learned from Clemente to share," Gonzalez said. "I have God-given abilities, and as a player and a human being I have a responsibility to take a message to the people."

After winning his first home run title in 1992, Gonzalez became the island's most popular and generous major leaguer. His status is not only due to his sudden fame and wealth. Gonzalez has remained a man of the people. He often pays medical bills or water and power bills for the needy. He still plays stickball in the streets, works out at a local gym, and offers batting lessons for Little Leaguers. "The people need someone like Juan," said the Cleveland Indians' Carlos Baerga, who also donates time, money, and heart to the people of Puerto Rico. "They look to baseball players for hope . . . that they can someday have a better life, too."

Puerto Rico is a small island of 3,425 square miles with a population of 3.5 million people. It is roughly the size of Connecticut, though far different in quality of life and economic status. Puerto Rico is afflicted with poverty, unemployment, drugs, and crime. As of 1994, one out of every five families received welfare. The unemployment rate was 20 percent, as compared with 5.5 percent in the mainland United States. The poverty level stood at 59 percent, compared with 13.5 percent in the United States, and the per capita income for Puerto Ricans stood at $4,177, compared with $18,696 for mainland residents.

Since the Great Depression in the 1930s, Puerto Rico, a commonwealth of the United States, has struggled to gain financial strength. While it does not have the poverty level of other Caribbean countries such as Haiti and the Dominican Republic, Puerto Rico has depended on the United States for financial assistance in building factories, buying tobacco and sugar, and allotting federal monies for schools, roads,

With high-rise buildings looming in the background, the shanties of the poor line the banks of a canal in San Juan, Puerto Rico. During the 1990s, Puerto Rico suffered a host of social problems, including widespread unemployment, crime, and drug abuse.

and social programs such as Medicare. Despite efforts by U.S. companies since World War II to do more business in Puerto Rico (taking advantage of cheaper labor costs), the three constants in Puerto Rican life have remained unemployment, crime, and drugs.

"There are many problems and they don't get help," Gonzalez has said. "Drugs are everywhere. People don't have jobs. People say I shouldn't go down there but I have to do something. Those are my people."

The game of baseball has been the island's one relief from all the troubles that surround everyday life. American soldiers stationed on the island after the Spanish-American War in 1898 brought the game to Puerto Rico. Because of the island's warm weather, youngsters were able to play the game year-round. The sport's popularity took off during the early stages of the Great Depression, when the financially strapped Puerto Rican government recognized the importance of baseball to the morale of the people. The government built what later became known as Sixto Escobar Stadium, named after the world bantamweight boxing champion from Puerto Rico. A six-team league formed, and more stadiums sprouted on the island. Huge crowds attended the games, and for a few hours each week the people were able to forget the real world.

The first Puerto Rican baseball hero was Perucho Cepeda, father of Orlando. Perucho Cepeda was a star on the island in the 1920s and 1930s. He won batting titles the first two years of the Puerto Rican League—he batted .465 in 1939—and played winter ball with legendary Negro league stars such as Hall of Famers Josh Gibson and Satchel Paige. Although he was clearly a great player, Cepeda never got a shot at the big leagues because of his dark skin. "Father never came to the states because of the race problem," his

Perucho Cepeda won the Puerto Rican League batting title in 1939 with a phenomenal .465 average. Despite his brilliance on the diamond, Cepeda was denied a chance to play in the major leagues because of his skin color.

son said. "Negroes were having a tough time then. Father had a bad temper. He would get mad. He would fight. He would have been thrown in jail if he came here to play. He used to say that."

The first Puerto Rican to play in the big leagues was a skinny right-handed pitcher named Hiram Bithorn, a native of Santurce. Bithorn joined the Chicago Cubs in the spring of 1942, benefiting from a shortage of talent while many big leaguers were serving in the armed forces during World War II. The major leagues scouted and signed players throughout Latin America, particularly Cuba, to fill out big league rosters, with one significant restriction: Latin players could not be signed if their skin was too dark. It was also understood that once the regular players came back from war duty, the Latin players would be sent home or demoted to the minor leagues.

During the war years, many of the Latin players experienced their first taste of American racism. Bithorn was no exception, although he was a white Puerto Rican. A junk-ball pitcher who relied more on his smarts than his arm to get batters out, Bithorn was hit hard early in his first season. He was heckled and cursed by fans and opponents. He wondered on many occasions what inspired people—even his own teammates—to such hatred.

Despite the abuse he had to endure, Bithorn was not going to pack up and go home to Puerto Rico. He was determined to prove he belonged in the big leagues. In the beginning he was used mostly as a relief pitcher, posting a 9-14 record for a Cubs team that finished sixth out of eight teams in the National League. Toward the end of that first season, the Cubs decided to try him as a starter. He completed 9 of his 16 games started, finished with a 3.68 earned run average (ERA), and proved to manager Jimmie Wilson that he should be part of the team's starting rotation in 1943.

Bithorn became the Cubs ace in 1943, going 18-12 with seven shutouts and a 2.59 ERA. Early that year the Brooklyn Dodgers added the second Puerto Rican in the majors, outfielder Luis Olmo, to their roster. It appeared likely that Puerto Rico, like neighboring Cuba, would soon have many players in the big leagues.

But Bithorn and other Puerto Ricans were drafted into U.S. military service. Bithorn did not pitch in 1944 or 1945. When he returned to the Cubs in 1946, he was 30 years old and did not have the same tireless arm he had shown before the war. Bithorn pitched mostly out of the bullpen in 1946 and 1947 before he jumped to the Mexican League. (He was assassinated in Mexico on New Year's Day, 1952.) As it turned out, it would be four years before another Puerto Rican player, Luis Marquez of the Boston Braves, would make the major leagues.

Not all Puerto Rican players thought reaching the big leagues was so important. By the time the war was over, the terrible stories of racism in the States, particularly among major league players, were known by everyone. The Brooklyn Dodgers finally broke baseball's color barrier in 1947, when they promoted second baseman Jackie Robinson to the big league club. But the Latin American countries were not pushing players toward the majors. Racism toward black Americans was out in the open, and Robinson was able to meet it head-on. But as Bithorn and others had learned, the prejudices shown toward Hispanic players could be just as deep and in some ways even more cruel.

In August 1948, representatives of Cuba, Puerto Rico, Panama, and Venezuela created a tournament of champions for each country's expanding winter league programs. In some ways, the quality of play—especially after the loss of so many young lives and potential ballplayers during World War II—was better in Latin America than in the United States. In addition, the Latin players did not have to deal with the racism and poor living conditions that they endured in the States, and they were able to express their ability without any distractions. The Caribbean World Series, as it became known, drew 25,000 fans for its debut in Havana, Cuba, in 1949. The series alternated between Cuba, Puerto Rico, Panama, and Venezuela over the next 12 seasons and showcased Latin America's talent to a suddenly open-minded major league baseball establishment.

If there is such a thing as a renaissance period for Puerto Rican baseball, that period was the early and mid-1950s. Puerto Rico's competition with its Caribbean neighbors led to an intense desire among Puerto Ricans to excel at baseball. Major league scouts such as Joe Cambria, Howie Haak, and Al Campanis realized the advantages gained by playing baseball in the warm Caribbean weather year-round. They knew that high schoolers in the Latin countries would generally be far ahead of their U.S. counterparts. Scouts began signing players throughout the Caribbean, particularly in Cuba and the Dominican Republic. While the scouts were responsible for signing players and sending them to the United States, broadcaster Buck Canel and New York Giants outfielder Willie Mays changed baseball in Puerto Rico forever.

Canel, who was elected to the Baseball Hall of Fame in 1985, arrived in Puerto Rico in 1946 to announce baseball after a successful career at NBC Radio in New York City. To his surprise, he was already famous on the island, for it was his voice that had translated the speeches of major political figures such as President Franklin D. Roosevelt to Hispanic listeners throughout Latin America.

Canel's true love was baseball. He had announced in the United States for 42 years and did so with a clear, mellifluous voice, in the most precise Spanish. Canel's linguistic achievement was remarkable because although he had been born in Argentina he had been raised in the United States and had taught himself Spanish. His was the voice that brought baseball into Latin Americans' lives, helping to connect them with a world of glamour and excitement. His trademark phrase was "Situación Don Q." The makers of Don Q, a popular brand of rum manufactured in Puerto Rico, paid Canel $100 to plug their product on the air. Whenever a player hit a grand slam, Canel would announce the blast as a "Situación Don Q," that is, an event that called for a glass of the sponsor's rum. Before long, Puerto Ricans were using "Situación Don Q" to cover all matters of life, as in, "Traffic looks bad today. We're in a 'Situación Don Q.'"

Willie Mays arrived in Puerto Rico in the winter of 1954, after winning the National League batting title and dazzling baseball fans with a spectacular over-the-shoulder catch in the World Series. No major league player of Mays's talent or fame had ever played in the Puerto Rican winter leagues. Mays was paid $1,000 a month plus expenses, a princely sum by Puerto Rican standards, and he proved to be worth every penny. Fans flocked to every game his Santurce Cangrejeros (Crabbers) played.

Santurce won the winter league title, and Mays captured the batting crown. While Mays played center field, a 19-year-old minor leaguer named Roberto Clemente was in left field. Clemente was in awe of Mays, not merely for his ability but also because of the way he handled fame and treated people. For his part, Mays found the young Puerto Rican a willing student. Among other things, Mays taught Clemente how to beat a pitcher at his own game of intimidation. "He suggested I get mean and if the pitchers knocked me down, get up and hit the ball," Clemente once recalled.

By the time Mays arrived, Puerto Rico had begun exporting players to the major leagues. Pitcher Ruben Gomez joined the New York Giants in 1953 and won a game in the 1954 World Series. Outfielder–first baseman Vic Power started 124 games for the Philadelphia Athletics in 1954, and the Cincinnati Reds promoted reserve outfielder Nino Escalera the same summer. In 1955 the Giants signed Perucho Cepeda's son Orlando, who reached the big leagues in 1958 and was the National League rookie of the year.

Puerto Rico could not have had two more different superstars than Cepeda and Clemente. Cepeda was an immediate hit with the fans in San Francisco and a team leader for the Giants, Cardinals, and Braves, all of whom won titles with Cepeda in their clubhouse. He hit 379 career home runs, tying him with Cuba's Tony Perez for the most by a Latin American player. He won the National League Most Valuable Player Award, made the All-Star team seven times, and

New York Giants star Willie Mays, photographed in the uniform of the Santurce Cangrejeros (Crabbers) during the 1954–55 winter league season. Mays's presence helped draw attention to Puerto Rican baseball, and a number of players from the island soon entered the major leagues.

posted a .297 lifetime batting average. If not for a serious knee injury in 1965, he would have surely finished his career with more than 400 home runs.

Unlike the soft-spoken, easygoing Cepeda, Clemente had an emotional edge that made him one of the most misunderstood players in baseball. He pushed himself to succeed on and off the field. He spoke out against racism and discrimination with a sense of confidence rarely shown by the Latin American and black players of his day. Though he could be moody and unapproachable with the press, he was always popular with the fans and always showed people the respect he believed all humans deserved, regardless of skin color.

"Latin American Negro ballplayers are treated today much like all Negroes were treated in the early days of the broken color barrier," he said in an interview. "They are subjected to prejudices and stamped with generalizations. Because they speak Spanish among themselves, they are set off as a minority within a minority. And they bear the brunt of the sport's remaining prejudices." That was not what America wanted to hear in the early 1960s. But the words were a revealing truth that endeared him to all Hispanics.

"You know, Clemente felt strongly about the fact that he was a Puerto Rican and that he was a black man," Buck Canel said in a 1976 interview. "In each of these things he had pride. But it was a beautiful, uncompromising kind of pride, because I never heard him—and you must remember that I am fluent in Spanish—I never heard him make a slurring remark about anyone's color or religion. In this he was remarkable.... He wanted very much to prove to the world that he was a superstar and that he could do things that in his heart he felt he had already proven."

The Dodgers originally discovered Clemente at a 1950 tryout and signed him in 1954, just after he graduated from high school. He spent one year in the Dodgers system before the Pittsburgh Pirates took advantage of a special ruling on minor leaguers and acquired his contract. The Pirates put Clemente, only 20 years old, right into their starting lineup and found him to be immensely gifted, if sometimes overly sensitive.

One day a New York sportswriter went to interview Clemente. "Roberto, you had a fine day and a fine series here," the writer began. "As a young fellow starting out, you remind me of another rookie outfielder who could run, throw and get those clutch hits. Young fellow of ours, name of Willie Mays." Clemente, not understanding that the writer was paying him a huge compliment, paused to think over the question and said, "Nonetheless, I play like Roberto Clemente." The writer assumed that Clemente was being arrogant.

The chance of misunderstandings between the media and Latin players is just as great today as in Clemente's day. During the 1993 season, for example, Juan Gonzalez expressed the frustrations of a three-game slump by attacking the bat rack. Aware that some observers would misinterpret this display of temper, Rangers manager Kevin Kennedy pulled Gonzalez aside for a talk. "Nobody ever said you can't get mad," Kennedy told his player. "It's how you come

Orlando Cepeda, Perucho Cepeda's son, realized his father's unfulfilled dream when he broke in with the San Francisco Giants in 1958. Over 17 big league seasons, the smooth-fielding first baseman batted .297 and hit 379 home runs.

back after that. You don't want to do something where it gets out of control or becomes detrimental to all your positives. What comes across as selfishness is really a matter of pride."

Like the young Clemente, Gonzalez found a way to take out his frustrations on the baseball. In the two games after his tantrum in the dugout, he went 5 for 6 with a home run in each game.

"It's very hard for Latin American players," Gonzalez said. "Why? Life changes completely, another language, another culture, you leave your family behind and you've got to become a man when you're young—by force. The first year was hard—no, not only the first, but the first three or four—before you feel comfortable in the culture here. But then you have the desire to make it, and it just carries you to get here."

Clemente would have understood those sentiments. He felt cheated by the baseball writers in 1960 after he helped lead the Pirates to the world championship over the New York Yankees. During the regular season, he had batted .314 with 16 home runs and a remarkable 19 assists from right field. He had hit safely in all seven games of the World Series. Yet, he finished eighth in the Most Valuable Player Award voting. Two teammates, shortstop Dick Groat and third baseman Don Hoak, finished first and second in the voting.

Clemente believed that his efforts had not been respected by the writers who cast their ballots for the MVP Award, and he was not afraid of saying so. As a result, the U.S. media branded him as selfish. Again, it was a classic conflict of cultures. "Latin society defines the individual in terms of dignity, in contrast to the North American definition, which focuses more on freedom and independence," wrote Michael and Mary Oleksak in *Béisbol: Latin Americans and the Grand Old Game*. "Each Latin guards his inner dignity. He will not be rushed. He will not be insulted, nor will he do anything he feels is beneath him."

The proud Clemente channeled his energies into making up for the slight he received. In 1961, he won the batting title with a .351 average and was named a starter in the All-Star Game. He also won batting titles in 1964, 1965, and 1967. He finally won the MVP Award in 1966, when he batted .319 with 29 home runs and drove in 119 runs. He averaged .328 during the 1960s and was without peer as a right fielder. He won a Gold Glove for his defensive play every year from 1961 to 1972.

While line drives rocketed off his bat and baserunners rarely dared to run on his powerful arm, Clemente was not fully accepted by the media or understood by his non-Latin teammates until the later days of his career. In 1971, at age 37, he batted .341 and led the Pirates to the pennant. He then put on an awesome display during the World Series against the Baltimore Orioles, batting .414 with two home runs, a triple, two doubles, and seven singles. He threw out one runner at home plate and nearly nailed another at third, after which the Orioles stopped trying to run on him. Suddenly, he was a hero in the United States. He began to receive attention for the work he did in Puerto Rico, like giving clothes, food, and money to the needy, conducting free baseball clinics, and playing winter ball in Puerto Rico every year to please the fans, although his tired body needed rest.

Clemente's tragic death inspired many Puerto Rican ballplayers to carry on his ideals. A sports complex, Ciudad Deportiva (Sports City), was built in his honor in Carolina, Clemente's hometown. Many children have developed their skills in many different sports at the complex. Since Clemente's death, there have been some excellent Puerto Rican baseball players: pitcher

Ed Figueroa, outfielder Jose Cruz, and first baseman Willie Montanez among them. But only since the early 1990s has Puerto Rico begun to produce players who have the talent to follow Clemente into the Hall of Fame. Cleveland's Carlos Baerga became the only big league second baseman other than Hall of Famer Rogers Hornsby to bat .300, collect 200 hits, hit 20 home runs, and drive in 100 runs in a season. Toronto's Roberto Alomar quickly became an All-Star second baseman and Gold Glove winner. His brother, catcher Sandy Alomar, Jr., was the 1990 American League rookie of the year. Ivan Rodriguez, Gonzalez's teammate on the Rangers, won two Gold Gloves before he was 22 years old. And Ruben Sierra, who ushered in the current crop of Puerto Rican stars when he broke in as a 20-year-old outfielder for the Rangers in 1986, has always dedicated himself to the memory of Clemente by wearing his number 21.

There are a number of reasons for this explosion of talent. "Baseball is our national pastime, more so than in many places in the USA," Luis Mayoral explained. "Since 1980, Ted Turner, with his TBS and CNN networks, has revolutionized the news industry. He helped tear down the Berlin Wall, disintegrate communism, and take baseball to Puerto Rico visually. People on an island 100 miles long by 35 miles wide can see over 700 games a year. It used to be that Puerto Rico and Latin America didn't have all these baseball magazines on the newsstands, *The Sporting News, Baseball America,* and these kinds of publications. Compared to other places in Latin America, we have been blessed with our association with the USA. If you go to Puerto Rico you'll see many places that are similar to the USA. You'll see many of the same things." In the midst of this heightened baseball awareness, Juan Gonzalez came of age.

After his tragic death in a plane crash on New Year's Eve, 1972, Roberto Clemente was immediately enshrined in the Baseball Hall of Fame. He remains a national hero in his homeland, and a number of Puerto Rican major leaguers have worn Clemente's number 21 as a way of honoring his memory.

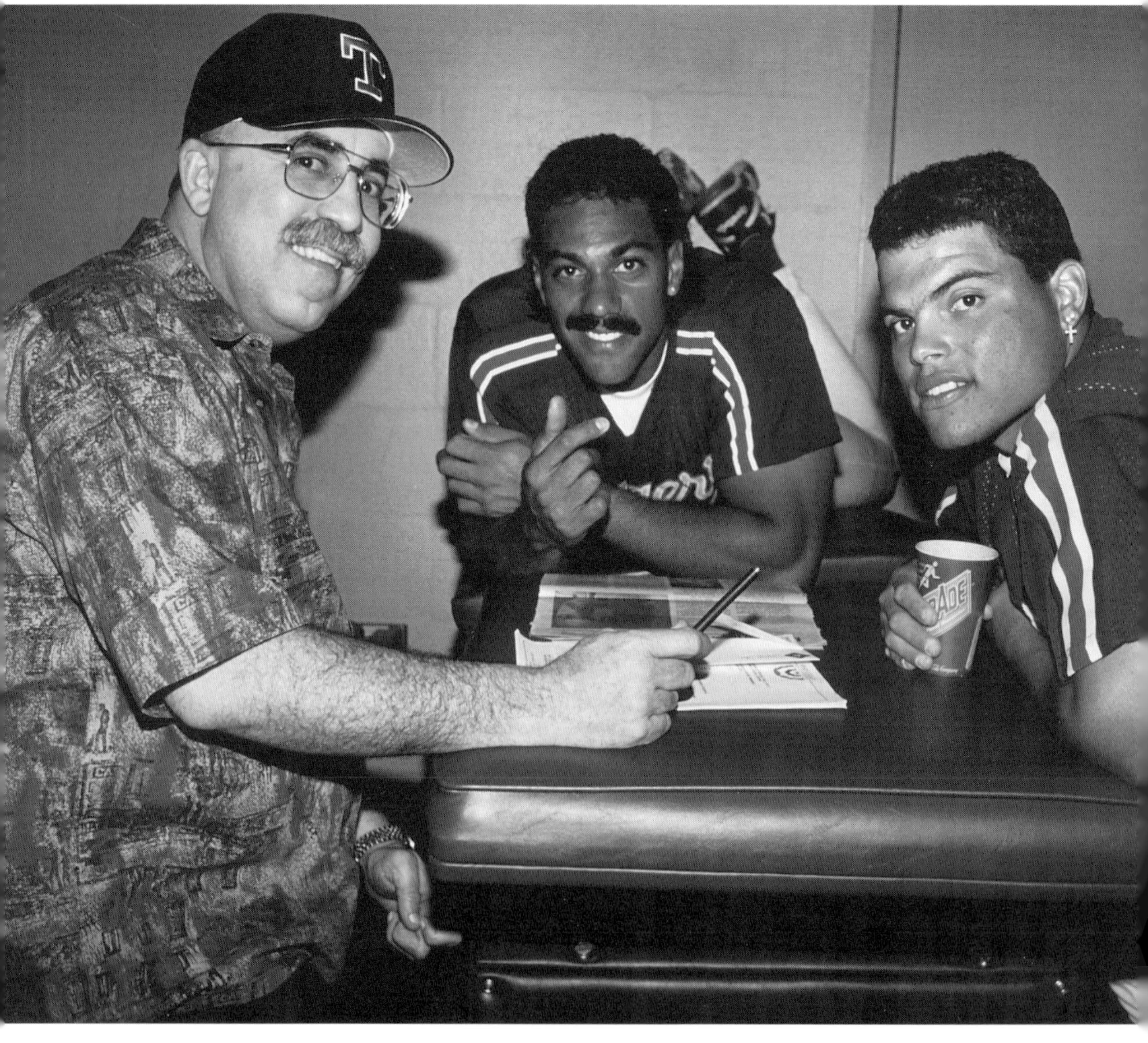

CHAPTER THREE

SOMETHING SPECIAL

Juan Gonzalez was tall, thin, and quiet when he was signed by the Texas Rangers in the spring of 1986. He stood 6 feet 3 inches and weighed only 175 pounds, and he certainly did not look like the next Orlando Cepeda. But he had long arms, a quick bat, and big, strong hands. And he was only 16 years old.

"I can remember playing against Juan when we were 13 or 14," said Carlos Baerga. "He was a good player, but nothing like he is today. He was a line-drive hitter and he was real skinny. A beanpole. I thought he could probably make the big leagues. I didn't think he would become such a home run hitter."

But Rangers scout Luis Rosa and assistant general manager Sandy Johnson believed Gonzalez had all the physical tools to be a great power hitter. "When I first saw Juan, he was 16 and a gangly kid," Johnson recalled in a *Sports Illustrated* article. "But he had the big frame, and you could tell he was a good athlete. He had tremendous bat speed, long arms and a natural power-hitter's swing. We felt right from the beginning we had something special. Honestly, what he has done is not all that surprising."

From the very beginning Gonzalez appeared to be a baseball-blessed child. He was born on October 16, 1969, the day the miracle New York Mets finished off the highly favored Baltimore Orioles in one of the biggest World Series upsets in history. Gonzalez was raised in Vega Baja, a town of 58,000 people just west

Texas Rangers stars Juan Gonzalez and Ivan "Pudge" Rodriguez pose with Rangers official Luis Mayoral in 1994. Gonzalez and Rodriguez were best friends while growing up in Vega Baja, Puerto Rico, and spent countless hours playing baseball.

of Puerto Rico's capital, San Juan. In Latin American countries the mother's maiden name is added to the name of a child, so Gonzalez's full name is Juan Alberto Gonzalez Vazquez. Since the age of 10, however, Gonzalez has been known to friends and family as Igor. As a child, he loved professional wrestling, and he became particularly fond of a wrestler named "The Mighty Igor." "I always wanted to be like him," Gonzalez recalled. "So I started to tell people that I was 'Igor the Great.'" Before long, even his parents were calling him Igor. When Gonzalez's son was born in 1992, he named the child Juan Igor.

In many ways, Juan was an ordinary Puerto Rican child who loved to play ball. There were very few ball fields in Vega Baja and only makeshift equipment. If the children did not own a bat they would use broomsticks. If they had no baseball they would use bottle caps or, as Gonzalez laughingly recalled, "the head off one of my sister's dolls." The game usually took place between buildings or on narrow streets. "Juan was like any other kid in Puerto Rico," said his mother, Lelé, "playing stickball on the streets or any other games little boys play. After he came home from school he was always playing baseball with his friends and had to be dragged home."

Juan grew up in a poor barrio (*barrio* is the Spanish word for "neighborhood") called Alto de Cuba (Cuban Heights). Until 1980, Vega Baja was known for its sugarcane. When the town's sugar industry started to decline, crime and poverty began to surround Juan's barrio. People begged for food and money in the streets, and many houses were old and crumbling. Filth littered the pavements, and the elderly were afraid to come outside. On the street where Juan grew up, drug dealers would operate in broad daylight because the police rarely came into Alto de Cuba.

Ten-year-old Juan Gonzalez (standing, fourth from right) poses with other members of his Little League team in 1979. Despite his skinny build, Juan's long arms and fluid swing indicated his potential as a power hitter.

When a police cruiser happened to venture into the area, it usually rushed away.

As the neighborhood grew worse, Juan's father became more concerned about his family's safety and the impact drugs and crime could have on impressionable children. Juan was 12 when his family moved two miles north to a safer neighborhood. "When we moved the family from the Alto de Cuba barrio, the reason was to get a bigger and nicer place," said Juan senior. "The drug problem was not so bad as it is today with the drug sellers all over the streets and the abandoned houses full of drug addicts. The Gonzalez family has had the same values and virtues typical of a low- to middle-income family ... always looking for the best for the family."

Juan junior differed from many youngsters in Alto de Cuba because his parents taught him the importance of discipline, education, hard work, and respect for others. Juan senior, a college graduate, was a public school math teacher who earned extra money by building houses. Lelé Gonzalez worked in a General Electric factory in addition to caring for Juan, his two younger sisters, and an older brother, named Juan Alberto Gonzalez Roman, from his father's first marriage. "[Juan] never had any bad experiences that affected his childhood," his mother said. "And his social consciousness was taught at home." Her son agreed. "I had a good home where morals played a very important role," he said. "My parents taught me that you can get ahead in life if you do honest work. You'll live a good life."

Growing up, Juan also played basketball and volleyball as well as baseball. "I began playing baseball when I was 6 or 7 years old," he remembered. "It was street ball in Vega Baja, and I also played *chapitas,* which is a game like baseball played with bottle caps. This game has always been fun to me. I always enjoyed baseball. I would play barefoot in the streets. I also like professional basketball games and wrestling, but baseball has been the number one sport in my life."

Like most boys who love baseball, Juan had his heroes. Puerto Ricans instinctively admire the great Roberto Clemente the way Americans idolize Babe Ruth; as time passes, the legends of both players only grow larger and more intriguing. But Juan also had more modern baseball heroes, such as outfielder Dave Winfield, then of the New York Yankees, and fellow Puerto Rican Jose Cruz of the Houston Astros.

"When I saw Winfield, I saw this big, tall guy who hit with power and moved well in the outfield," Juan said. "I projected myself to be like him." His first impressions of Cruz date to his 11th birthday. "I remember Jose Cruz cried at the end of that famous

Dave Winfield, who starred for the New York Yankees during the 1980s, was one of Gonzalez's favorite major leaguers. "I projected myself to be like him," Gonzalez recalled.

game," he said, recalling Game 5 of the 1980 National League Championship Series, one of the best playoff series ever. Each of the first four games went into extra innings, and the Phillies and Astros squared off for the decisive contest in Houston's Astrodome. The Astros had a 5–2 lead in the top of the eighth when the Phillies scored five times. Then Cruz tied the game with a two-run single in the bottom of the inning. Again the teams went into extra innings, and the Phillies won the pennant in the 10th. Cruz, a quiet, distinguished man, cried openly after the defeat. "When I saw Cruz in the dugout," Juan said, "it got to my heart."

As it turned out, Cruz later became a big factor in Juan's giant leap into professional baseball. In the winter of 1986, the veteran and the youngster played the outfield together for the Ponce Lions. Cruz, who never received due credit for collecting 2,251 career hits, was always admired by his teammates for being a team leader and class gentleman. "He was the only major league player that gave me confidence when I was young," Juan said. "He told me how to lead my life, basically how to take care of yourself. He helped me a lot. He gave me advice about the game and life."

Cruz was one of the first big league players Juan met. But he had no idea that his best friend and constant playmate was going to be a future All-Star and Gold Glove winner. Rangers catcher Ivan "Pudge" Rodriguez is two years younger than Gonzalez, and he made the big leagues for good almost two years sooner. As children, the two were virtually inseparable. "I would go to his house and say, 'Juan, let's go out and play baseball,'" Rodriguez recalled. "We'd go out in the front and play and pass time. We did the same thing at school. We had a lot of good times and we'd talk about games and other things, like reaching the major leagues. We've always had a good relationship."

Like Baerga, Rodriguez was amazed that Juan grew to be so big and strong. Rodriguez was always fairly short and a little husky. He realized early on that becoming a good catcher might get him to the big leagues, but Juan played the outfield and pitched. "We hit the ball hard," Rodriguez said. "We didn't hit many home runs because the parks in Puerto Rico are so big. A line drive in the gap would roll to the fence for an inside-the-park home run. But we weren't hitting many of those big, long home runs."

"I was very skinny," Juan recalled. "I did not have the power until I turned maybe 13. I hit a lot of hard line drives. Generally, I was a good Little League player. I pitched once in a while but not regularly. While playing Mickey Mantle ball for the town of Vega Alta, the manager made me an outfielder."

Juan was 14 when he played for Vega Alta, and he had already caught the eye of two scouts, former big leaguer Vic Power of the California Angels and winter league manager Orlando Gomez of the Rangers. "You could see the talent," Gomez said. "He was skinny and tall, but he was that type of skinny you could see he was going to build up and get strong."

As Juan started to grow, so did his appetite. "I ate beans, duck, goose, rice . . . real Latin food," he said with a big laugh. Among the scouts who were looking at players such as Rodriguez, Baerga, and Roberto Alomar, word was spreading fast that Juan was developing into a home run hitter. In fact, the New York Yankees stumbled onto outfielder Bernie Williams when they were scouting one of Juan's Mickey Mantle League games. "They definitely knew about Juan when they came to see us play," Williams recalled.

"I was around 15 when I started to think one day I would play major league baseball," Juan said. "I may have thought about it before. But at that age I began to understand that I had a great chance of doing it. If there was something that could have helped me decide to go for it, it was a three- or four-homer game I had."

As the story goes, Juan's father answered a knock at the door one evening and found his 15-year-old son standing in the doorway with his coach.

"What do you feed this kid?" the coach said.

"Why are you asking?" Juan senior replied.

"He hit three mammoth home runs today," the coach said. "It was incredible."

From the look on the coach's face, Juan's father realized his son might be a major league prospect. He

Jose Cruz of the Houston Astros drives a grand slam home run into the bleachers at Chicago's Wrigley Field in August 1984. One of the finest all-around players of his era, Cruz gave advice and encouragement to young Puerto Rican players such as Gonzalez.

was right. Before long, scouts from the Rangers, Blue Jays, Angels, White Sox, and Yankees started showing up at Juan's games.

"The first thing we look for in 14-year-old and 15-year-old kids is the throwing arm," said Rangers scout Luis Rosa. "Then we look for soft hands. Then we check their builds. If they can hit, that's a bonus."

When the scouts began to make offers, Juan senior handled the negotiations. The Rangers and Blue Jays offered almost the same terms: a $75,000 signing bonus. The elder Gonzalez also insisted on a college scholarship worth $34,000. Juan junior decided that all things being equal, he wanted to play for the last-place Rangers because he thought that would be the easiest route to the major leagues. "I just thought it would be better to join a last-place but growing organization looking for help," he later said.

When Rosa went to the Gonzalez home to finalize the signing, he found that Juan's father wanted more money. Rosa would not go any higher. Juan and his parents went into the kitchen to talk over the contract offer. They returned a few minutes later, Rosa recalled. "He was outvoted two to one," Rosa said of Juan's father. "When I signed Juan, I told a TV station I just signed the top home run hitter to come out of Latin America. When the books are closed on his career, he could reach 500."

Juan's signing bonus was the richest ever given to a Latin American player. But Rosa, who had scouted in Puerto Rico for 10 years, was confident his latest discovery would live up to the large investment. "Let me assure you Juan Gonzalez is the finest prospect to come out of Puerto Rico in years," he told a Dallas reporter.

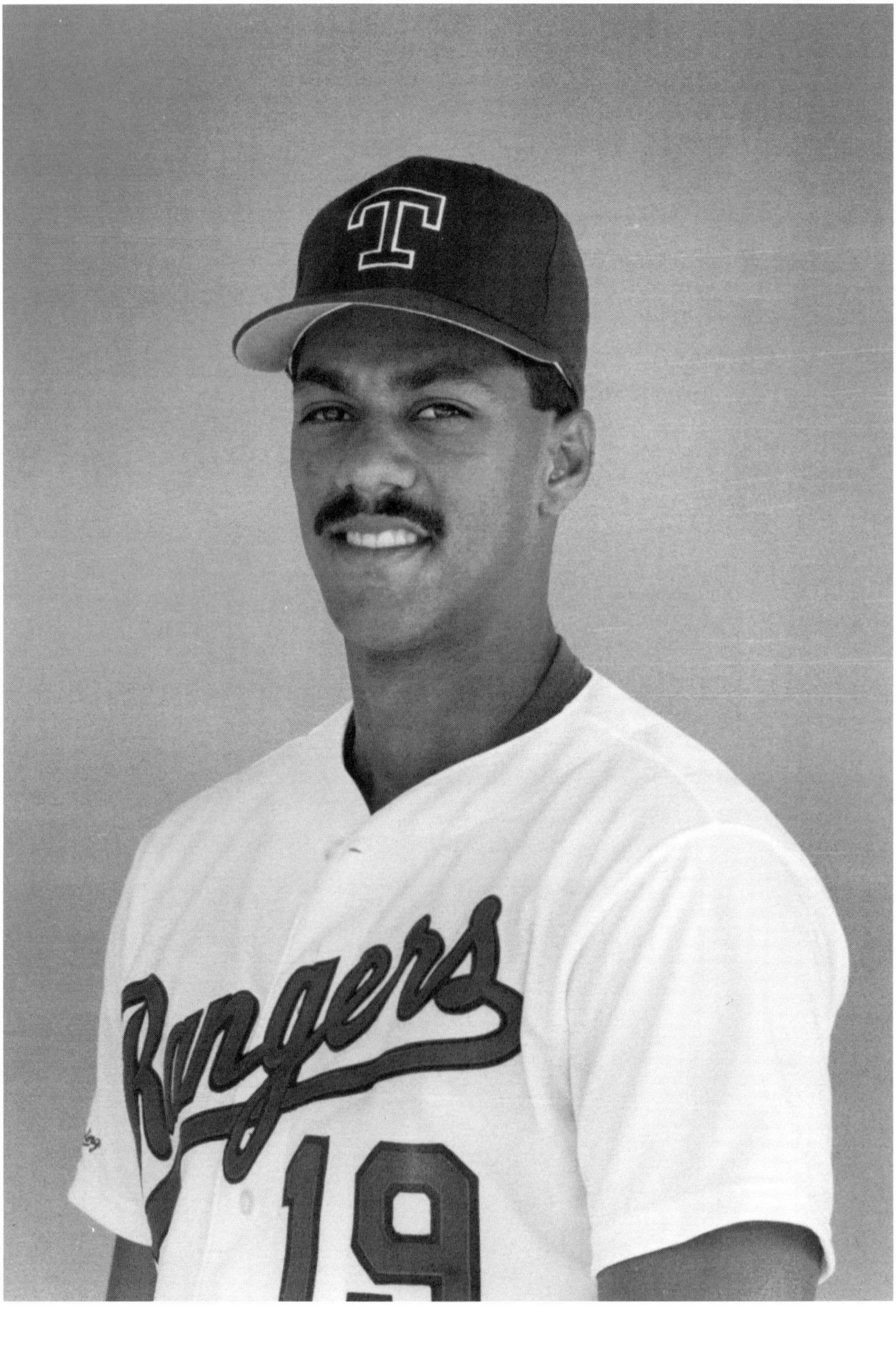
Rangers
19

CHAPTER FOUR

NEW CULTURE, NEW LANGUAGE

In the minor league system that develops players for the majors, there are four levels of competition. The rookie league plays only about 60 games a summer. Then come Class A, Class AA, and Class AAA, all of which play 144-game seasons. At a time in life when most boys his age were still seniors in high school, Gonzalez was beginning his professional baseball career. It was June 1986, and he was four months shy of his 17th birthday. He was scared and lonely, and he started to miss his family and friends before he ever left for the United States. But once he reported to Sarasota, Florida, and the Rangers' Gulf Coast League rookie team, he realized there were 24 other players just as scared, just as lonely, and just as determined to one day reach the major leagues.

Gonzalez wanted to prove quickly that the Rangers had not wasted their bonus money on him. Most of all, his intense pride would not allow him to return home a failure. He never doubted he had the ability to play professional baseball. But he soon saw how much harder he had to work and how much more he had to learn. The Sarasota Rangers had about 15 excellent prospects on the team, including future big leaguers in shortstop Rey Sanchez, hard-throwing pitcher Kevin Brown, outfielder Sammy Sosa, and third baseman Dean Palmer. Like Gonzalez, all had signed right out of high school. Gonzalez quickly realized that many

As a young prospect in the Texas Rangers organization, Gonzalez had a long, hard climb to the major leagues. In addition to developing his baseball skills, he had to learn English and adjust to a foreign culture.

other players had as much talent as he did at that stage of his career, if not more.

"Baseball is really hard," he said in looking back on his years in the minor leagues. "A lot of people think you just pick up a bat and glove. But before you can do that, you have to work very hard. You have to practice all day, every day, to improve your game because nothing in life is easy, least of all baseball. Baseball is a game of suffering, but baseball is beautiful. You enjoy it. You're entertaining thousands of fans. To get there you have to work hard, to sacrifice yourself."

The coach at Sarasota was a fair and sensitive man named Rudy Jaramillo. He understood what the young players were going through by being away from home for the first time. But he also knew that playing baseball was now their job, and he wanted to make sure the new professionals took their job seriously. "We were always making them aware of what they were there for and where they could go," he said. "I don't know if we did all the right things. But looking back, we knew they were talented kids. We just gave them information and advice. They're the ones who observed it and put it between the lines. They had to have the mental capacity to adjust to this new way of life."

Jaramillo served as a cross between being the players' big brother and their biggest nightmare. Off the field, he helped the boys handle outside factors, such as adapting to American society and homesickness. "I was constantly talking to them and getting them to be comfortable," he said. "We picked them up in vans in the morning, we would be at the complex all day, and we brought them home. We'd go to the gym three or four times a week. We'd go out to the mall or to eat dinner. We'd sit around and talk baseball. Repetition of that, talking the game of

Texas general manager Tom Grieve, a former major league pitcher, was one of Gonzalez's greatest boosters. "When we saw Juan for the first time," Grieve said, "[we knew that] if ever there was a guy who was going to be a star, he was going to be that guy."

baseball about such things as game conditions, helped get them in the frame of mind to do their jobs better."

But Jaramillo also could be demanding and tough. He pressed the players hard and pushed them to their limit in the blistering Florida summer. He taught them about conduct and practice habits, told them how to stay out of trouble, and reminded them of what they needed to do on the field to become big leaguers. He expected discipline on and off the field, and he wanted to instill strong work habits that would carry his players throughout their career. "In a sense, I was real hard on them," he said. "I remember Sammy Sosa telling me one time, 'You're worse than the sun because you're like the devil.' That's one thing that was hard for them. We had a lot of discipline. None of them was too used to that."

Jaramillo immediately saw why the Rangers felt Gonzalez was such a good prospect:

> You saw the arm and the bat speed.... He didn't have any kind of foot speed to mention, and he was real uncoordinated at first. He was just a skinny ol' rail, maybe 6-1 or 6-2, and 175 pounds. It was a real hard adjustment for him. He didn't really drive the ball that first year, but there were things you could see in batting practice. You just had to look at the raw skills. When you saw him day-in and day-out, you'd see the brilliance, you'd see something there. He hadn't matured, but in batting practice you'd see the raw power. Dean Palmer was another one like that. At times he was unbelievable. It's just that Gonzalez's coordination hadn't caught up with him. When he played in games he'd just find some holes and put the ball in play. The biggest part with him is like any other 17- or 18-year-old: being away from home the first time. He got down on himself real easy. But I never heard him say he wanted to go home, although I know he

got homesick. He was an immature kid, which is what you expect of someone that age.

"At first, he felt a little nervous because it was the first time he was going to leave home and be separated from the family," Gonzalez's mother said. "He used to call home, . . . seldom to say that he wanted to come back, but to tell us that everything was okay and he was playing well. Our advice to Juan was to do his job, learn everything that they taught him, and never get into trouble with the justice."

"My family was back home and I was homesick," Gonzalez recalled. "I called home every day. But I never thought of going back. I missed my family, but I had a goal. I had it in my mind I wanted to make the major leagues. I knew I'd have to go through this. I never let down, although I got discouraged."

Gonzalez's first professional season was the least productive of his five minor league campaigns. He failed to hit a single home run in 60 games, and 51 of his 56 hits were singles. His slugging percentage was a terrible .266—although he led the league in at-bats with 233. "The thing you saw about him," Jaramillo said, "was that any time people were in scoring position, he had a knack for driving them in. I thought that was something special for someone being 16 years old. He liked to be in that position."

Gonzalez led the league with 36 runs batted in. But he also led the team in temper tantrums. "He was hot-tempered," Jaramillo added. "But he was just frustrated that he wasn't doing as well as he should be. He pouted when he wouldn't hit the ball as well as he could. Then, the discipline and other stuff we constantly talked about came in. More than once I remember having talks with him, and I can remember being very strong with him. That worked only because of the communication we had and the trust we had for one another. I told him the truth. I explained

NEW CULTURE, NEW LANGUAGE 53

to him what wasn't right and the way he was going about his job was wrong. He needed to improve his work habits and stop getting down on himself."

Sammy Sosa agreed. He recalled having long talks with Gonzalez that first year, trying to help him conquer his temper, discouragement, and homesickness. "We talked a lot, sometimes late in the night," Sosa said. "We were young guys, and we knew we could play this game. We knew if we went out there and did our job and practiced hard every day, you would start to show your talents. After we got there we realized we had to go out there every day, work on our hitting, and take fly balls every day."

Back in Arlington, Texas, Rangers assistant general manager Sandy Johnson, general manager Tom Grieve, and the entire minor league office were raving about the crop of young players the team had signed and placed at Sarasota. A reporter for the Dallas *Morning News* decided to visit the rookie league team and see whether the talk was fact or fiction. The Rangers had finished last in the American League West Divi-

Gonzalez poses for a photograph with Tony Scruggs (left) and Sammy Sosa at the Rangers spring training camp in 1988, when all three were striving for a shot at the big leagues. "We were young guys, and we knew we could play this game," Sosa recalled.

sion in 1984 and 1985, and if these young players were as good as the big league team was claiming, the paper wanted to give fans a look into the future.

When the reporter got to Sarasota in late July, Gonzalez, Palmer, and Sosa had combined to hit only three home runs in over a month's worth of games. Although Sosa was putting up some good numbers en route to batting .275 with 19 doubles and 96 total bases, the reporter focused his article on Gonzalez. He cast Gonzalez as a struggling, homesick youth who had cost the team almost 10 times more in bonus money than most of his teammates had received. Coach Jaramillo, a veteran of handling nervous and lonely young players, was quoted as saying, "everyone is just trying to survive here. No one cares where everyone came from. It's where they are going that's important." His optimism was vindicated when 11 players from that 1986 Sarasota team eventually reached the major leagues.

If the Rangers had evaluated Gonzalez's, Sosa's, and Palmer's future on that first year, they all would have been sent home. They struggled to adjust on the field and off—and it was especially tough on Sosa and Gonzalez. While they became good friends and leaned on each other during troubling times, they were still just boys. Neither had been prepared for the different lifestyles and expectations of being a professional baseball player in a foreign country. And since many of their teammates and opponents were up to five years older, they were often overmatched in games. Moreover, neither of them could speak a complete sentence in English.

"It was horrible," Sosa said. "When you come to this country the first time, you don't know anything. It was hard for me. It was hard for all of us. You go into McDonald's and you don't know how to order what you want to eat. We always had to go with somebody

NEW CULTURE, NEW LANGUAGE

Gonzalez and third baseman Dean Palmer had disappointing seasons at Sarasota in 1986, their first year as professionals. Five years later, however, both players were established major leaguers. "To get there you have to work hard, to sacrifice yourself," Gonzalez reflected.

who spoke English. We didn't want to go alone because we didn't want to get into trouble, you know, people misunderstanding us. We didn't know how to say anything."

"The only ones who understand how difficult it is to play in those conditions are those who go to winter ball [in Puerto Rico or Venezuela], and it's thrown into their lap that they have to survive in a different country," Jaramillo added. "The culture, the language, going somewhere to eat. Because you don't speak the language you feel like someone is talking about you, and you get paranoid about that. When you're 16 or 17 and you've never been away from home and then you start to struggle a little bit on and off the field . . . well, I'm not sure people sometimes understand."

Gonzalez looked back on that first year in amazement. He never expected the Latin and North American cultures to be so different, and he certainly didn't expect such difficulty in adjusting. When he left Vega Baja for Sarasota, the language and cultural problems were distant issues compared with the challenge of playing professional baseball. "Cultures are different," he remarked. "American kids are stimulated to look out more for themselves. In Puerto Rico, the parents are a little more protective. The emphasis in the USA is mostly on education, earning money and working hard. For Latin players it is difficult to adapt to life in the USA."

Gonzalez admitted that he resisted the idea of living differently and learning a foreign language. But his coaches, friends, and family finally convinced him that he would have to make the adjustment if he wanted to succeed in major league baseball. "When I became a pro player and all of a sudden saw that a great part of my future would be spent in the USA, I really understood the importance of learning English," he said. "It would help me in communicating with the media, in marketing, et cetera.... It's hard for all Hispanics. What you learn back home in English is just the basics—mother, father, sister, the money, good morning, how are you."

The Rangers felt Gonzalez needed to learn English, but they also wanted him to make physical progress during the off-season. They put him on an extensive weight-training program and assigned him to the instructional league—a 40-game season played at the Rangers complex in Port Charlotte, Florida, during the winter. "We'd like to see him spend a minimum of one full season at Class A, Class AA, and Class AAA levels," Sandy Johnson said. "We are in no rush. Hey, by the time the kid is 21, he will have been a professional for five seasons."

Coach Jaramillo was given special instructions for the team's future power hitters: work them, and work them hard. "I remember Sandy Johnson coming in and telling me that he wanted this instructional league to be like a boot camp. I went and cut all my hair off, being like a drill sergeant," the coach said.

NEW CULTURE, NEW LANGUAGE

Throughout his career, Gonzalez has struggled to control his temper after failing to deliver at the plate. As a young player in a strange country, his frustrations on the field were often aggravated by feelings of homesickness.

The Rangers' weight-training program included a very basic exercise—jumping rope. "It was a very strenuous jump-rope program," Jaramillo recalled. "They hadn't been in anything like that. I felt like the jump rope would give them stamina and get them better coordinated. Juan certainly needed better foot speed and coordination."

Gonzalez had never really spent much time in the weight room, but pumping iron and working out proved to be relaxing and enjoyable. Just as the scouts had predicted, Gonzalez suddenly started to grow. He went from 175 pounds to a more muscular 190 during the off-season. As his next minor league coach, Chino Cadahia said, "It's unbelievable how good they can get in just one year."

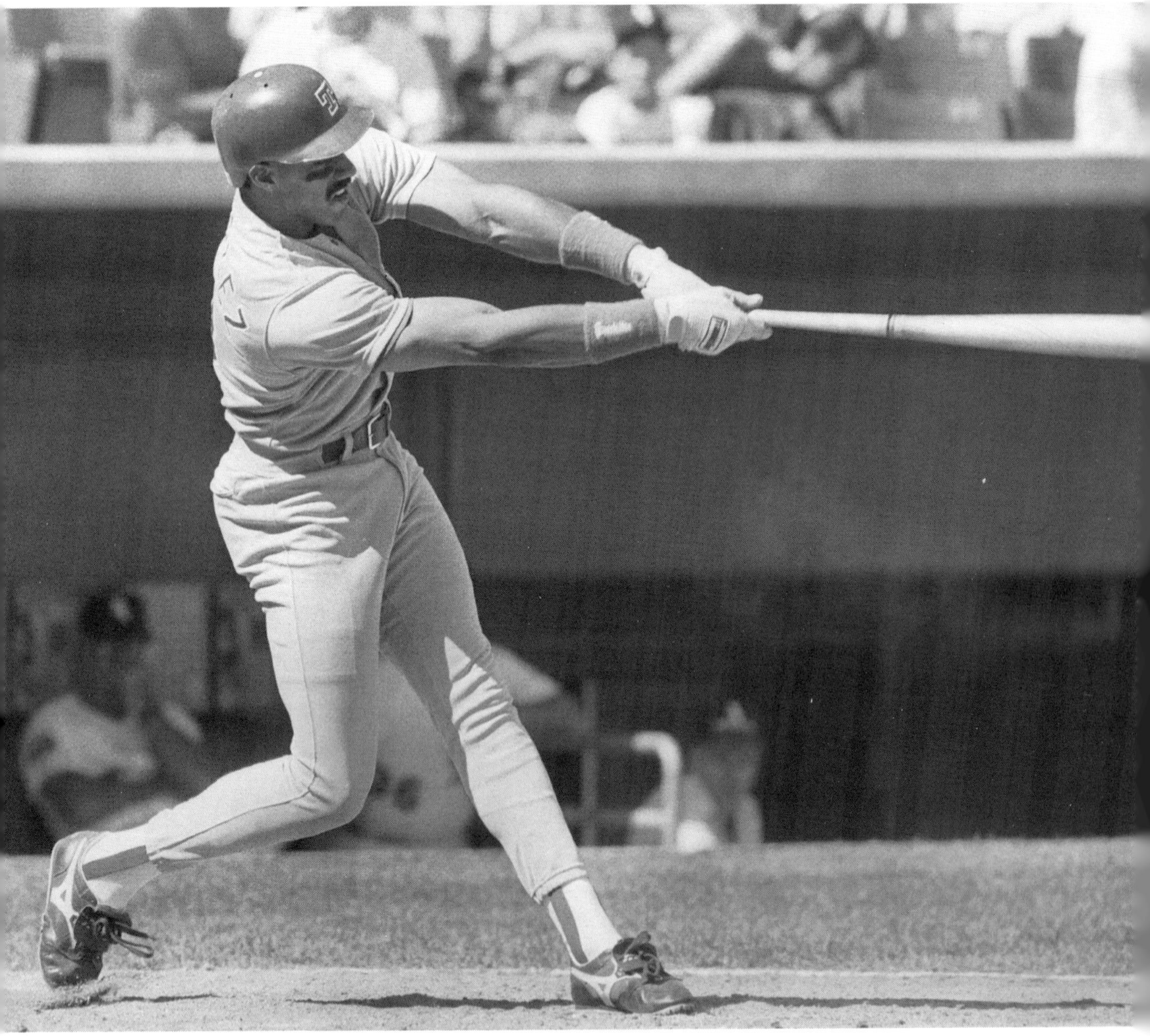

CHAPTER FIVE

IGOR THE MAGNIFICENT

The baseball world got its first glimpse of Gonzalez's potential during his second pro season. He returned from a winter of weight training and instructional league ball stronger and more advanced as a player. The Rangers then sent Gonzalez, Sammy Sosa, and Dean Palmer to their Class A Gastonia, North Carolina, team in the South Atlantic League. "Besides being a year older and a year wiser, Juan was a little stronger, too," said Gastonia manager Chino Cadahia. "I saw him in instructional league that fall. By the time he got to me, he was physically so much stronger. You could really start to see the power in him."

Gonzalez's iron pumping was pushing his weight toward 200 pounds, and he could already see the difference at the plate. Where he used to hit hard line drives to the warning track, now the ball started flying over the fence. His swing, bat speed, and coordination all started to come together. At age 17, he was physically catching up with many of the older players who had several more years of college and professional experience.

"Kids in the USA eat better than kids in Latin America and Puerto Rico," Gonzalez said. "They have better opportunities to practice baseball and other sports. So at maybe age 17 they get better and bigger than us. However, up until 16 or 17, players in Puerto Rico are much better because due to our

Gonzalez smashes a home run against the White Sox in Chicago's Comiskey Park. "From the hitting standpoint, everything just seemed to click with him," said Texas coach Tom Robson. "He did it so effortlessly, so easy, and then boom!"

A series of Juan Gonzalez baseball cards depicts a classic power hitter's swing. Throughout his minor league career, Gonzalez continued to add muscle to his 6-foot-3-inch frame: year by year, his home run totals climbed.

camp that spring was to make sure Dean Palmer, Sammy Sosa, and Juan Gonzalez get 400 at-bats. Those 400 at-bats taught those kids a lot. If you look at the track record of those three after that, every year they all got better."

In terms of Gonzalez's performance on the baseball field, the Rangers were glowing about the progress the young prospect had made in just one year. But an old problem kept coming back—his moodiness and homesickness. It was a problem that would follow Gonzalez all the way to the major leagues, and something only a visit from his family could cure. "Yes, we still give him advice and reprimand him if we need to," his mother said.

"I think the hardest adjustment at this level is just playing every day," added Cadahia. "They don't come from any program in the States or Latin America where they play every day, where they are having to get up every day and being ready to play, controlling their emotions and learning from every at-bat. Their moodiness is more mental than physical and it's just a part of growing up."

Gonzalez strove to be such a perfectionist that he would get angry at himself for his own failings. The best teacher of baseball is experience, and too often Gonzalez's experiences involved his immaturity. "After that 1986 season he was actually getting a bad rap about trying so hard that he wouldn't run out a ball if he failed at the plate," said Jaramillo. "He would pout like any young kid. We all do that at that age."

Gonzalez's progress at Gastonia in 1987 carried over to the 1988 season. He was sent to Port Charlotte of the Florida State League for another year of Class A training. He batted .256 with 8 homers and 43 RBI in an 80-game season, and there was no reason for the Rangers to keep him from moving up to Class AA in 1989.

"When Juan got to Tulsa," said manager Tommy Thompson, "he was still just a kid with a lot of ability. He was just starting to blossom. He had an above-average arm and above-average power. If you ever looked at thoroughbred horses and saw a 2-year-old, you knew if you had a Kentucky Derby horse. Let me tell you, he was just 18 years old at double-A ball and you could see he was going to the big leagues."

Thompson took the same approach as Jaramillo and Cadahia in handling Gonzalez. "I try to manage just like it's my family," he said. "I don't think it was as tough an adjustment here for Juan as it was his first couple of years. I started to see a lot of maturity on how he was supposed to approach the game and approach life. Double-A ball is a springboard for many players and Juan was one of those. He learned about the work ethic. He was driven. It's an inner thing, an inner drive that separated him from a lot of the others. He took lots of extra hitting and work sessions."

Before coming to Tulsa, Gonzalez realized that the major leagues were now within his reach. He worked harder in the weight room, and he concentrated on his weaknesses while playing winter ball. As the Class AA season progressed, two events brought him closer to his goal. In late June, when he had hit only 7 home runs, Gonzalez was hit in the face by a pitch. Rather than scaring him off the plate, the incident angered Gonzalez, and he took out his aggression on the baseball, hitting 14 homers in the final two months of the season. "I think he wanted to show people that it didn't bother him," Thompson said. "Some people never recover from something like that. Juan went the other way."

The other significant development came on July 29, when the Rangers traded Sammy Sosa, pitcher Wilson Alvarez, and infielder Scott Fletcher to the

Chicago White Sox for the aging but still productive outfielder Harold Baines.

Sosa had been quickly promoted from Class AA Tulsa to Class AAA Oklahoma City in the first three months of the 1989 season, and the Rangers brought him up to the majors on June 16. In his debut, he went 2-for-4 against the Yankees, and five days later, he hit his first major league homer off Boston's Roger Clemens. After 25 games with the Rangers, Sosa was batting .238 with 1 home run and 3 RBI, and the

Gonzalez rounds third base after belting another home run. When the Rangers traded Sammy Sosa to Chicago in 1989, the move created an opening for Gonzalez on the team's major league roster.

Rangers sent him back to Oklahoma City. The Rangers were not seeking to unload Sosa, but they found themselves surprisingly close to the powerful Oakland Athletics in the race for the American League West title. They felt they needed a proven hitter in order to make a run at first place and were willing to sacrifice some good young prospects in order to get the experienced Baines.

Many people criticized the trade because the Rangers had a long history of making moves for the short-term that backfired on them later on. A prime example was the 1982 trade that sent two of their top pitchers, Walt Terrell and Ron Darling, to the New York Mets for declining outfielder Lee Mazilli. Terrell was later traded to Detroit and became an important part of the Tigers' drive to the 1984 world championship and the 1987 American League East title. Darling became one of the stars of the 1986 Mets world championship team and one of the National League's best pitchers in the latter half of the 1980s.

So when the Baines trade was announced, many Rangers fans feared the worst. Baines performed well, batting .285 in 50 games for the Rangers, but Oakland captured the division anyway. Sosa became a promising but erratic performer for the White Sox. Alvarez pitched a no-hitter for the White Sox in 1991, and when the team rolled to the division crown two years later, he won 15 games. It was fair to say that the Rangers got the worst of the Baines trade. But Rangers fans later learned that it could have been much worse. In 1993, a reporter revealed that Gonzalez's name had come up during the trade talks with the White Sox. In the end, the White Sox had preferred Sosa because they thought he was much closer to being a major league player.

The trade of Sosa essentially opened a position for Gonzalez on the Rangers, when he was ready. When the team slipped out of the pennant race in the second half of the 1989 season, the Rangers called up Gonzalez and Palmer from Tulsa on August 29. Gonzalez's farewell at Class AA was a solo home run against the Jackson Mets. He finished his Class AA season with 21 homers, 85 RBI, a .293 batting average, and a robust .506 slugging percentage.

"We needed a boost at that time," said Tom Robson, then the Rangers' hitting instructor. "We brought up a bunch of kids. Palmer was 20 years old. We called up Pudge Rodriguez to catch in the middle of the year, and he was just 19. Juan was only 21."

General Manager Tom Grieve told the Tulsa *Tribune* about Gonzalez: "He's still just a kid. But we thought enough of him to sign him when he was 16. If he develops as we expect, he has a chance to be a superstar and the best player—the best player by far—we have ever signed."

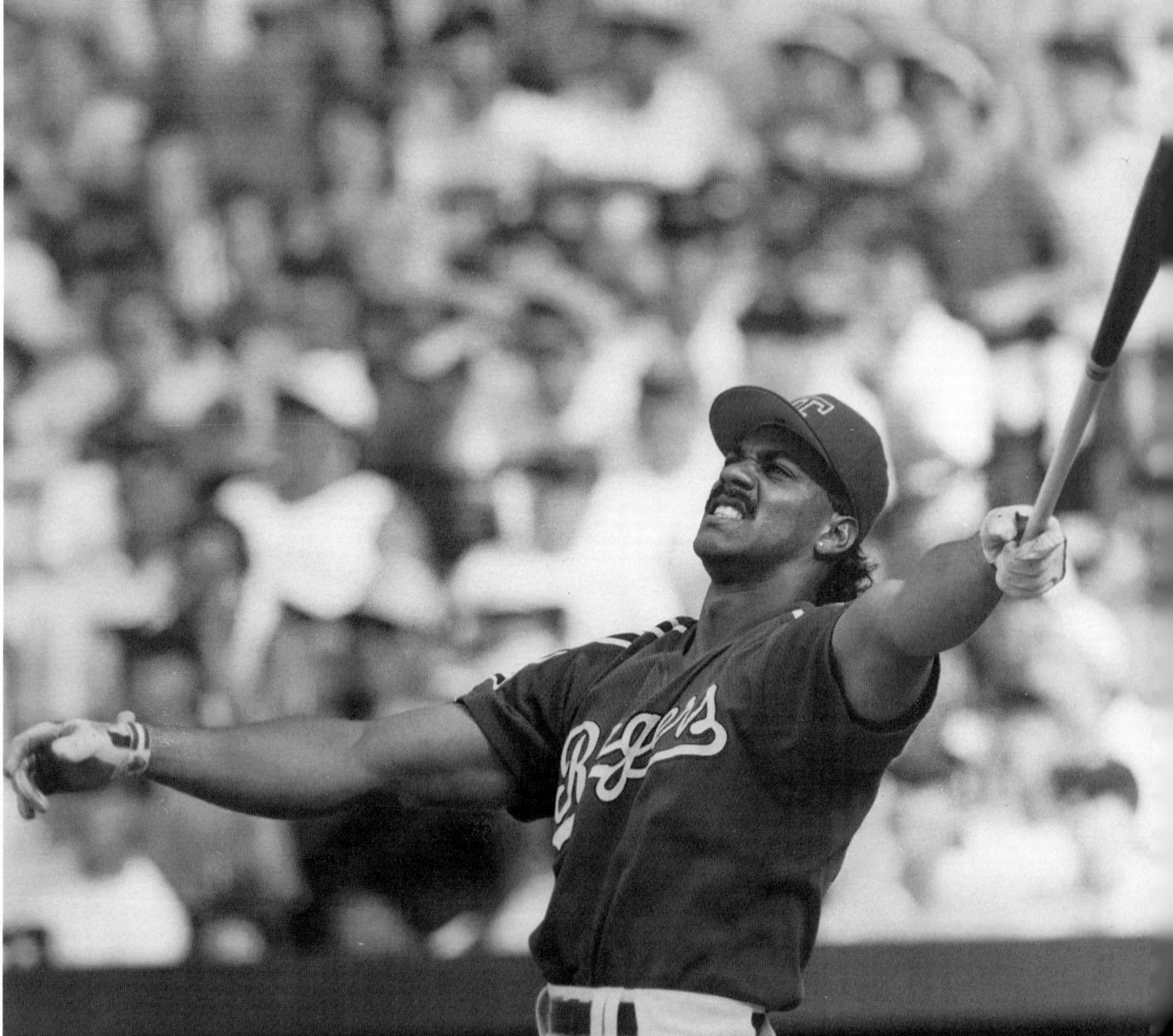
Rangers

CHAPTER SIX

HOME RUN KING

Much to Gonzalez's unhappiness, his stay in the major leagues lasted only for the final month of the 1989 season. The Rangers placed him in center field for 24 games, and that was plenty of time for manager Bobby Valentine and hitting coach Tom Robson to observe the team's most valued prospect.

"He was very undisciplined, maybe trying too hard," Robson said. "He was trying to hit balls out of the park he couldn't possibly hit out. He misjudged some balls, made some baserunning mistakes, and tried to hit the ball too hard with two strikes. These were all things we wanted to see ourselves. This was a time when we had only heard about him and it gave us a chance to evaluate his abilities."

Gonzalez desperately wanted to make a good impression. "I was very excited to be in the major leagues," he said. "I don't think I was all that nervous. I just wanted to show them what I was capable of doing. It was a real proud moment for me, but I was proud for Pudge, too.... Here we were, from Vega Baja, a small town in Puerto Rico, and both in the major leagues and both with the Texas Rangers."

Along with Rodriguez, Gonzalez found instant friendship and guidance from the team's other Latin players: first baseman Rafael Palmeiro, designated hitter Julio Franco, and outfielder Ruben Sierra (a native of Rio Piedras, Puerto Rico). Palmeiro remembers Gonzalez's first month as being a typical adjustment

Gonzalez watches one of his shots sail out of Baltimore's Camden Yards. In 1992, the Texas slugger became the sixth-youngest home run champion in baseball history.

for any player, with the added burden imposed by Gonzalez's lack of English. "He was young and real shy," Palmeiro said. "He didn't say much and he didn't speak English very well. He always seemed mature and you knew he was going to be a good player. You could see it. You could see he had some power."

Gonzalez showed flashes of his potential in that one month in the big leagues. His batting practices were very impressive, and Tom Robson said it was obvious he was still growing. Gonzalez was 6 feet 3

Rafael Palmeiro, one of several Spanish-speaking players on the Rangers roster, helped Gonzalez adjust to life in the major leagues.

and 215 rock-hard pounds. And people kept forgetting this boy-giant was just 19 years old. "Juan, as a player, had the luxury of having a phenomenal amount of ability in his body," Robson observed. "The one advantage he had over other hitters was he didn't have to hit it correctly for it to go out of the park. When he hit it correctly, everyone just stared."

One of those people was pitcher Scott Bankhead, then with the Seattle Mariners. On September 18, 1989, Gonzalez hit his first major league homer off Bankhead, at Arlington Stadium. It was a long, impressive blast, and it turned out to be the only home run Gonzalez hit in his first stint in the majors. His trial run with the Rangers resulted in a .150 batting average with just 7 RBI and 17 strikeouts in 60 at-bats. Gonzalez was disappointed, but the Rangers were not.

"I don't think we ever thought about not sending him back to the minors," said Valentine. "But he didn't take failure very well. The games where he struck out more than once were particularly rough on him. I was constantly walking by his locker just to see if he was keeping his head up. Ruben Sierra did a pretty good job with him to keep him up. In the end we just felt that maybe he needed a little more time."

By the end of the 1989 season, the Rangers had not made a decision on where Gonzalez would spend 1990. Gonzalez was determined to make the big club in spring training. He played winter ball and worked out religiously at the gym. One of the things the Rangers learned from Gonzalez's month in the majors was that he would likely be better in left field than in center. When spring training opened in 1990, the Rangers were giving Gonzalez every chance to stay in the majors.

"I think he probably expected to make the club," Robson said, and the coach was right. Gonzalez felt he was ready, even without Class AAA experience. By the end of spring training, however, the Rangers felt that a year in AAA would help Gonzalez. They sent him to Oklahoma City, where he enjoyed his best minor league season with 29 homers, 101 RBI, and a .508 slugging percentage. He still struck out 109 times in 496 at-bats, but his power numbers had improved dramatically. When the Rangers called him back to the big leagues in September, Gonzalez made up his mind that he was not going back to the minors again.

"We knew it was only a matter of time before he got back to us," Robson said. "He just needed to polish up his game a little bit. We knew he was coming back. We also knew that once he got back, he was there to stay forever."

Gonzalez played 25 games in the last month of the 1990 season and had 4 homers, 12 RBI, a .289 batting average, and just 18 strikeouts in 90 at-bats. He was only 20 years old, but he seemed significantly more mature than he had a year before. Now he seemed destined for the stardom that had long been predicted.

Gonzalez, indeed, would never go back to the minors. "That second year, he came back and he was ready to show us something," Bobby Valentine said. "He had spent a lot of time in the weight room, and I saw where he worked out in his little hometown. The guy in the gym there said he was there every day, sometimes four or five hours."

A year later, after Gonzalez's first full season in the big leagues, Valentine made a winter trip to Puerto Rico. He was attending the wedding of Rangers pitcher Edwin Correa, but Valentine took the opportunity to check up on some of his players, including pitcher Jose Guzman, who was trying to come back from a shoulder injury. He also wanted to gain insight into Gonzalez. "I went to Juan's home and met his mom and dad and tried to break the barrier and get a little closer," Valentine said. "It was obvious he was a

Bobby Valentine, Gonzalez's first manager in Texas, took a personal interest in the rookie, even visiting his family during the off-season. "It was obvious he was a special athlete and a special guy," Valentine said.

special athlete and a special guy. We made a lot of special efforts to make him feel at home and [to let him know] that the organization cared about him."

Gonzalez was coming off an impressive rookie season in 1991. He batted .264 with 27 homers and 102 RBI, and many believed he should have been the American League rookie of the year. But Gonzalez had too many at-bats in 1989 and 1990 to qualify as a rookie in 1991. Minnesota Twins second basemen Chuck Knoblauch achieved wide notice when his team won the World Series by defeating the Atlanta

Braves in an exciting seven-game series. As a result, Knoblauch won rookie of the year honors even though he hit only 1 home run and drove in 50 runs, while making 18 errors in the field.

The suggestion was made that Gonzalez failed to gain much national attention in 1991 because he spoke so little English. Though Sammy Sosa had been quite correct when he said, "When you hit the ball, you don't have to speak English," a player does have to speak English to North American reporters, who vote on the awards. And because Gonzalez was shy around non-Latins and still struggling with his English, many writers did not even bother to talk to him after games. "When you're Latin American playing in the United States, you have to deal with all the factors—including a dramatic personality and the language barrier," Bobby Valentine said. "At the beginning, Juan didn't want to speak English. He was fine when we would be together [Valentine speaks Spanish]. But I got the feeling like he was never going to allow anyone to laugh at his English. It was very difficult for him, but then, he had a good supporting cast around that was in the same boat."

"It's terrifying to someone like Gonzalez only when you have to do interviews and he doesn't understand the question or what's going on," said Rafael Palmeiro. "As far as the game itself, it is played the same everywhere in the world. I knew he was going to be fine on the field. It's off the field, whenever you have to go somewhere, do interviews, or talk to kids that's difficult."

Gonzalez's performance that season was also overshadowed by the feats of pitcher Nolan Ryan. As Ryan's remarkable 27-year major league career was winding down, the media became more obsessed with him every time he took the mound. In one regard, having Ryan on the team took a lot of pressure off

HOME RUN KING

Nolan Ryan signs autographs after a spring training workout. The media's obsession with Ryan, baseball's all-time strikeout king, enabled Gonzalez to develop his skills without being hounded by reporters.

Gonzalez, because the media was so wrapped up in his every move. The highlight came on May 1, 1991, when the 44-year-old Ryan pitched the last of his seven career no-hitters, against Toronto. As the season wore on, newspaper and TV reporters followed Ryan everywhere, wondering what else he might accomplish and speculating as to whether he was planning to retire. At that stage of his career, Gonzalez was happy to play in the shadow of a legend.

After the 1991 season, Tom Robson wanted Gonzalez to continue to make improvements. He was concerned more with the player's approach to the game than with his technique. Robson believed Gonzalez had an efficient swing: his hands rotated properly, his weight shift was good, and the energy he generated from the feet and thighs up to the hands was excellent. "He looked so effortless when he hit," the coach said.

To progress as a hitter, Gonzalez needed mainly to think about what he was doing at the plate. "Every day you talk about hitting will help get them in the right mental frame of mind," Robson continued. "If you overload them, they can't get into that groove thing. You have to learn to know what to expect from pitchers each day, whether he'll bust you with the fastball or take you with a breaking ball away. You've got to be prepared. We tried to keep him relaxed."

Gonzalez listened, and he responded with a monster year in 1992. He found his home run swing midway through the season and hit 24 round-trippers in the second half. He went through terrific stretches. He had three homers against Minnesota on June 7, and he had three two-homer games within five days in July. In another hot streak, he homered in four consecutive games.

As the season went on, Gonzalez found himself battling Oakland's Mark McGwire for the American League home run crown. The Oakland slugger had started off fast, but a rib cage injury forced him to miss 20 games in August and September. Gonzalez took advantage of McGwire's absence and passed him on September 11, when he hit his 40th homer. McGwire came back and tied Gonzalez a week later as Gonzalez went into a slump.

"[Gonzalez is] going to the plate with the idea of hitting it over the fence," Rangers coach Orlando Gomez told the *Los Angeles Times*. "You can't blame a guy, this time of year. He's going for it. He really wants to finish ahead."

However, Gonzalez was stuck at 40 for two weeks, and McGwire took the lead with his 41st homer on September 26. But Gonzalez came to life, hitting homers on consecutive nights in Oakland as the season came down to its final weekend. On the next-to-last day of the season, McGwire hit his 42nd in an afternoon game and tied Gonzalez again.

"He tied me?" Gonzalez said when he heard the news during the evening's batting practice, as the Rangers prepared to take on the Angels in Anaheim. "Well, I'll swing the bat tonight. I'm looking for number 43."

Gonzalez did not get his homer that night, but he was determined to take the home run title on the final day. He hit one out against crafty veteran Bert Blyleven, and when the day was over, he had the home run title with 43. The achievement, barely noted in the United States, touched off a wild celebration in Puerto Rico. While baseball purists were reminded of a young Reggie Jackson or Mickey Mantle when they saw Gonzalez's homers, the fans of Puerto Rico saw another Orlando Cepeda, the last Puerto Rican to hit 40 home runs in a season.

The title put Gonzalez in some of baseball's most elite company. At age 22, he was the sixth-youngest home run champion. Gonzalez's 109 RBI made him only one of five active players to have driven in 100 runs in their first two seasons; Jose Canseco, Wally Joyner, Don Mattingly, and Frank Thomas were the others. And Gonzalez was only the eighth player to have two 100-RBI seasons before his 23rd birthday. Having averaged 24 homers a year in his last three minor league seasons, Gonzalez was averaging 37 in his first two big league seasons.

The Rangers honored Gonzalez's season by naming him the team's most valuable player. In addition to his 43 homers, he had batted .260 (a respectable figure for a power hitter) and had a .529 slugging percentage. Realizing his value, the Rangers decided to renegotiate Gonzalez's contract, offering a four-year, $14 million deal. Gonzalez chose to play out the final year of his existing contract, although it called for a salary of $525,000. Clearly, he felt that he could do even better than $14 million in a year's time. "I'm doing my job, working hard every day. The money's in the bank," Gonzalez said with a laugh.

The off-season proved to be one of significant change for the Rangers and Gonzalez. He had married his high school sweetheart, Jackie Ortiz, and he became a father on February 13 when Jackie gave birth to a son, Juan Igor. At the same time, the Rangers were reshuffling their on-field management. Bobby Valentine and most of his staff had been fired during the 1992 season as the Rangers faded again in the second half. Gonzalez found himself especially

Gonzalez lashes a home run at Arlington Stadium in June 1992. As the season drew to a close, Gonzalez engaged in a stirring home run duel with Mark McGwire of the Oakland A's.

missing Tom Robson, who had always handled the sometimes temperamental slugger with a soft touch. Toby Harrah, a former coach, ran the team during the final two months, and he and Gonzalez often clashed. Gonzalez was painted as spoiled and brooding, and he was labeled a troublemaker. According to his teammates, this was anything but the truth. Gonzalez was only 22, and the other players did not expect him to have the maturity of a veteran player.

"Most Latin players are very sensitive," Rafael Palmeiro explained. "They are cautious of everything, so you have to be careful with a guy like Juan. Let him play ball. When he makes a mistake, leave him alone. He realizes what he has done. Nobody likes to be embarrassed. But Latins take it personally, whether it's constructive criticism or not. I understand what he's going through—I was that way myself, maybe not to that extent. The only pressure he's got is the pressure he puts on himself. He puts it on himself because he wants to be the best, he wants to be perfect. With the awesome talent he has, he just has to learn to chill out when he's struggling. You're always going to have hard times, you just have to stay on an even keel."

Gonzalez agreed. "The only Latin players who have no problem with language are those who came when they were kids," he told *USA Today Baseball Weekly*. "But those of us who came from our countries at 16 or 17, to learn the language at that age is a lot harder. For a reporter, it's hard to understand. For a Latin player, it's hard to express himself clearly to the press because he doesn't know the language perfectly. I don't want to do what I don't do well."

The Rangers were concerned about Gonzalez's frame of mind. They wanted him to improve his English, and they wanted him to stop getting so frustrated when he failed. But if they had to choose between Harrah and Gonzalez, they were not about to trade away a 22-year-old player with 75 home runs in just over two seasons. So they hired minor league manager Kevin Kennedy to run the team and let Harrah go. Perhaps the most important decision the Rangers made came off the field, when they hired longtime Puerto Rican sportswriter and sportscaster Luis Mayoral to work in their public relations office.

The Rangers hired Mayoral specifically to increase the team's presence in the Hispanic community and help the Latin players adjust to a new country and the North American media. The move was bold and smart, for the bald, chain-smoking Mayoral was instantly likable and fun to be around. He wore gaudy neckties and thick eyeglasses, and his good nature was always well received. He became the radio play-by-play announcer on the team's Spanish-speaking network while working in Hispanic communities during the day. In between, he was coaching the Latin players on behavior, adjusting to the United States, and handling the media.

Mayoral's presence in Gonzalez's life and career came at the perfect time. The media were growing more and more curious about the Rangers' emerging star, but few journalists could communicate with him. The Rangers understood—and Gonzalez's agent and business manager certainly understood—the importance of getting endorsements and media attention. But the Rangers also felt Mayoral could be like a big brother to Gonzalez, and Gonzalez's parents heartily endorsed the friendship. Gonzalez had never been one to get into trouble, but why wait for it to happen? Mayoral became Gonzalez's personal coach in matters of image, politeness, and emotional self-control.

"When you take a young man like Juan, sometimes it's difficult with the travel, the rigor of the baseball schedule, and the expectations of others," Mayoral said. "He also knows this profession brings

Gonzalez confers with Rangers deputy public relations director Luis Mayoral during batting practice. A seasoned sportswriter and broadcaster, Mayoral became Gonzalez's friend and confidant, helping him deal with the media and advising him on how to conduct himself on and off the field.

you good money when you are dedicated and succeed. There's also the chance you can run into the wrong crowd because of who you are. Juan is very well protected. He has an agent, a financial advisor, and he's got me. He learned long ago to be very selective with his friends."

Many have said Mayoral's calm presence helped lift Gonzalez to yet another level in 1993. But Gonzalez made a promise to Rangers coach Orlando Gomez in the final weeks of the 1992 season that he was going to improve his batting average and cut down on his strikeouts. "We had a long conversation about having bad games and having good games," Gomez said. "You have to learn that's going to happen."

Whatever the reason, Gonzalez was even better in 1993. He started with two mammoth home runs against Baltimore at Camden Yards on opening day, and he kept up his assault on American League pitching until the last day of the season. By the All-Star break, he had 23 homers and 60 RBI. He was also batting over .300 for the first time in his career, mainly because he worked at hitting the outside pitch to right field. As his average rose, pitchers found fewer holes in his swing.

He was not elected to the All-Star team by the fans, but he was selected to play on the team. Thus, his most telling moment was the dramatic home run–hitting contest in which he outslugged Ken Griffey, Jr.

Gonzalez continued his torrid home run pace after the All-Star Game. He finished with a .310 batting average, 46 homers, and 118 RBI—all in just 140 games. He hit his 100th career homer on July 16, gaining a tie with Joe DiMaggio as the 11th-youngest player (22 years, 9 months) to hit 100 home runs. (Mel Ott, at 22 years, 4 months, heads the list.) Gonzalez hit 20 homers over July and August and matched his 1992 total of 43 in early September. But just when it appeared certain that he would hit 50 home runs, a sore back kept him out of the lineup for almost the remainder of the season. Still, his total of 46 again led the American League and tied National League home run champion Barry Bonds of San Francisco for the major league lead.

Gonzalez became the first American Leaguer since Boston's Jim Rice (1977–78) to lead the league in homers in consecutive years. He was only the fourth major leaguer in the previous 23 years to have consecutive 40-homer seasons. Of his 46 homers, 22 tied the game or put the Rangers ahead. He had 11 game-winning home runs and 13 multi–home run games. He was also the 11th player in history to drive in 100 runs in each of his first three seasons.

Gonzalez now began to get recognition. He was named to the Associated Press Major League All-Star Team and to the *Sporting News* American League All-Star Team. He was third in the balloting for American League player of the year.

Throughout the season, Gonzalez remained humble about his own success as baseball bid farewell to teammate Nolan Ryan, who had announced in the spring that 1993 was going to be his last year. As the great pitcher traveled from city to city, he was showered with long ovations and fan appreciation. Gonzalez learned a lot by watching the easygoing, well-liked Ryan. Ryan handled the media in a way that rarely upset the writers, and he graciously accepted the fact that fans wanted to see him pitch and get his autograph before games. Ryan was particularly fond of children and involved himself in a number of charitable causes. All these examples made an impression on Gonzalez. While most people were becoming aware of Gonzalez's talents and vast potential on the field, very few—including Rangers officials—knew of the silent mission in his life. Gonzalez was determined to pick up where Roberto Clemente had left off 20 years before, and his efforts had been underway for nearly 3 years.

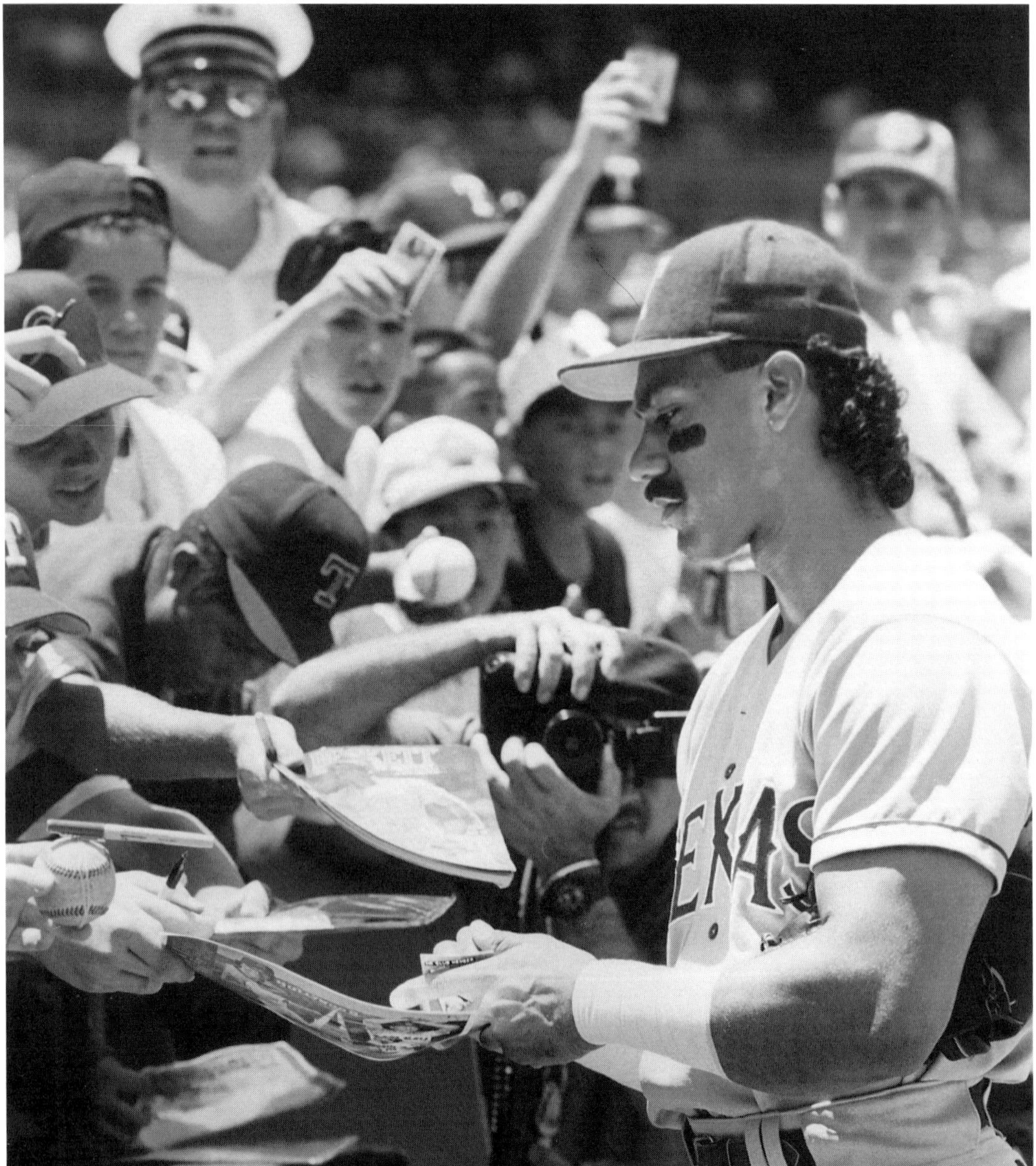
TEXAS

CHAPTER SEVEN

"HE IS A FRIEND TO ALL"

The perils of drug abuse were never far from Gonzalez's own life. His older half brother, Juan Alberto (usually known as "Puma"), was found dead of an apparent drug overdose in a public housing project in the spring of 1994. He had spent time in prison and a drug clinic. "I knew sooner or later something like this would happen," Gonzalez said.

Gonzalez had tried to lead his brother away from crime and drugs, just as he tried to encourage all children to go to school and listen to their parents. "Igor always looked for his brother at the drug-dealing place in Alto de Cuba and gave him money to buy clothing," said Gonzalez's mother. "He helped him a lot. Igor promised a car and a house to his brother if he gave up drugs. He supported him a lot and would give him money."

"I was surprised he died," Gonzalez recalled. "Right before his death he was in a rehabilitation center. Everything up to the time of his death was proving that down the road he was going to beat the addiction. He was on a one- or two-day pass from the rehab facility. You don't get a pass if you're not making progress, so it was a big surprise to me.

"It affected the way I played. I'd walk up to the plate and it was inside my mind," Gonzalez continued. "I'd be thinking, 'I've lost my brother,' instead of

A genuine superstar after his back-to-back home run crowns, Gonzalez signs autographs at Anaheim Stadium in 1994. Broadcaster Jim Palmer, a Hall of Fame pitcher, called Gonzalez "the perfect guy—the one that, if I were a youngster, I'd want to emulate."

concentrating on baseball. It was a problem for a long time."

His brother's troubles with the law and drugs had helped lead Gonzalez on a mission to help others long before Puma's death. Many of Gonzalez's friends had also died. Others had gone to jail. He had seen the crime on the streets in front of his house. But this did not prepare Gonzalez for the terrible news that his brother was dead. "I tried to offer help and advice, whatever he needed," Gonzalez said. "But he wouldn't take it. You can only do so much."

"Juan was very different," his father said, "because he was always under my advice, and Juan saw what drugs did to his half brother. He knew to stay away from drugs and stay in school and play baseball."

Gonzalez could not explain how he became so dedicated to his family and his homeland, but he knew that someone had to help others less fortunate than he was. "He's a kid who is very smart, very sharp," said another Puerto Rican hero, Orlando Cepeda. "He's concerned about his people and concerned about his community. He's very level-headed and he knows what he wants and what he needs to do for his community, his country."

Gonzalez was inspired by the great Roberto Clemente, and he was told by ex-players such as Cepeda that he should be the new torchbearer for Puerto Ricans. Like Clemente, Gonzalez loves children. He sees their parents using drugs and stealing to get money. He sees them without enough food, their clothes torn or without a park to play in. When asked what he would have been if he wasn't a baseball player, Gonzalez said, "a very good social worker."

Gonzalez came along at a time when the island needed a new hero, one for the younger generation. When he is in Vega Baja, he has been known to pay the utility bills or medical expenses of people in need.

Gonzalez poses with a group of teachers and students from Mi Escuelita, the school he sponsors in Dallas, Texas. At Mi Escuelita, Hispanic youngsters learn English so that they will be better prepared for elementary school.

He also throws an annual Christmas party in the streets. He has bought vitamins for youngsters at the local gym, and like Clemente he plays winter ball so Puerto Rican fans can see him play in person.

Wherever Gonzalez goes in Puerto Rico, there is a stir. Sometimes the experience of being recognized and admired is bittersweet for Gonzalez. Once, an admiring fan presented him with a hollowed-out seashell with a painting of Gonzalez inside. The fan insisted that Gonzalez meet the artist and led him down a path to an old shack. Inside, a group of men scattered as Gonzalez ducked inside. The shack contained many souvenirs and photos of Gonzalez. But the shack was also known as a haven for drug users; one of the men tried to hide all the needles so that Gonzalez would not see them. "What happens there makes me very sad," Gonzalez said.

Another time, Gonzalez stopped to hug a little girl in front of her house, on the very street where he grew up. People began to flock around him, running from their houses and waving their arms and screaming, "Igor! Igor!" But two doors down, a young boy, a drug dealer, stood in the doorway of an abandoned house. A man approached; the boy reached into a hole in the wall and handed the man a small packet. The man paid the boy, who added the money to a thick wad of $100 bills he kept in his pocket.

"It makes me feel bad and sad at the same time," Gonzalez told *Sports Illustrated*. "The youth is losing its future to drugs. But I also blame government authorities for not caring for the people of the barrio. . . . There is a saying in Spanish: 'We criticize but do not help.' That's what happens here."

Gonzalez appealed to the government to help, but usually he acted on his own. In the winter of 1994, the Rangers rewarded him for his play, vindicating his self-confidence. A year earlier, they had offered him $14 million for four years. Now they signed him to a seven-year contract worth a total of $45 million, making him one of the highest-paid players in baseball. One of the first things Gonzalez did was create a special commission to build a community sports center in his barrio. He also became more involved in the "Yo Sí Puedo" (Yes I Can) educational program and the Alianza para un Puerto Rico Sin Drogas (Alliance for a Puerto Rico Without Drugs), not to

"HE IS A FRIEND TO ALL"

At home in Puerto Rico during the 1993 off-season, Gonzalez visits a childen's home run by Sister Isolina Ferre (right). In addition to playing winter ball for the Puerto Rican fans, Gonzalez spends many hours talking to youngsters about the benefits of hard work and the dangers of drugs.

mention numerous other groups that help the needy. Gonzalez also formed a youth foundation that received the money he earned by appearing at baseball card shows. Gonzalez made a special effort to attend the card shows in cities such as Los Angeles and New York, where there are many Hispanic fans, realizing that they were eager to see Latin major leaguers.

"We're a motivation and inspiration to so many young ones back home," Gonzalez said. "They can see there are other ways to live than to get lost in drugs and other negatives in life. I have to do my best to prove to the youth that hard work can accomplish anything."

No one knows more about hard work and the harmful effects of drugs than Orlando Cepeda. At one time, he was as popular in Puerto Rico as Gonzalez later became. But shortly after he retired from baseball, he was found guilty of bringing marijuana onto the island. He went to jail for a year, and because of the damage to his reputation he failed to make the Baseball Hall of Fame.

"What happened to Orlando was a teaching to the world," Gonzalez said. "But it was also a teaching to ballplayers and people who are outstanding in life. You have to play the game of life correctly to see if it comes out right. Don't play it incorrectly to see if it comes out right. Do it the correct way."

After a long, troubling time, Cepeda regrouped and went to work for his old team, the San Francisco Giants. Like Gonzalez, he put his pleasant personality and love for children to work by going into poor neighborhoods, talking about the dangers of drugs, and visiting homeless shelters and the needy.

One day Cepeda invited Gonzalez to lunch. "I mentioned to him why he has to play winter ball for five or six weeks out of the year," Cepeda said. "He doesn't say yes or no. He just went back to Puerto Rico and did it. He's helping the whole island by playing. How many people have the money to come to the U.S. and see them [Puerto Rican big leaguers]? It makes a big impact and it's helping the whole island."

Soon, more top Puerto Rican players followed suit: Sandy and Roberto Alomar, Leo Gomez, Carlos Baerga, Edgar Martinez, and others. Fans turned out by the thousands to see them play. But the people came especially to see Gonzalez. Often during games, fans would run on the field between innings just to touch him or shake his hand. It was not unusual for him to sign autographs for an hour before the game and an hour afterward. One time, he drove for over an hour to a game that was eventually rained out. He stood on the muddy field for over 30 minutes signing autographs for children who were disappointed they did not get to see their hero play.

"This is a mission I have taken upon my shoulders," Gonzalez said. "At the same time, I am happy to break a barrier that existed for over 20 years. I'm glad to see the Baergas, the Alomars, and others helping out. Since Clemente, no one in Puerto Rico has really gone out for the people. My mission is to take a message out to the people, to inspire them and motivate them because since Clemente died, they think no one cared about them."

After the baseball season, Gonzalez typically speaks at about 50 schools each winter, telling the youngsters about the dangers of drugs. He conducts free baseball clinics for young players and walks the streets to see who needs help. Children swarm around him, and when he begins to talk, they all hush to hear their hero, who always provides words of encouragement. "When your mother and father talk to you, you should listen," he tells them. "Sometimes you get mad at them. That's natural. But you should be grateful to them, because a united family is the basic foundation for having a chance for a good life."

After he is done talking the children crowd around him again. He gives hugs, kisses, and autographs. Often he has to escape out the back door of a school to avoid the crush. But he knows that if his message reaches just one child, he might be saving a life.

In Puerto Rico, Gonzalez is relaxed and happy. He is with his family and friends. While playing baseball in the United States, he is often shy, private, and very focused. Gonzalez's parents taught him to take pride in his work, even if that work is playing a game. "We always tried to get him to show that other side," said former manager Bobby Valentine. But one of the turning points of Gonzalez's career and his growing popularity in the United States was a *Sports Illustrated* article in 1992 titled "Puerto Rico's New Patron Saint." Even people who knew Gonzalez well—including many with the Rangers—saw an aspect of the young slugger they did not know.

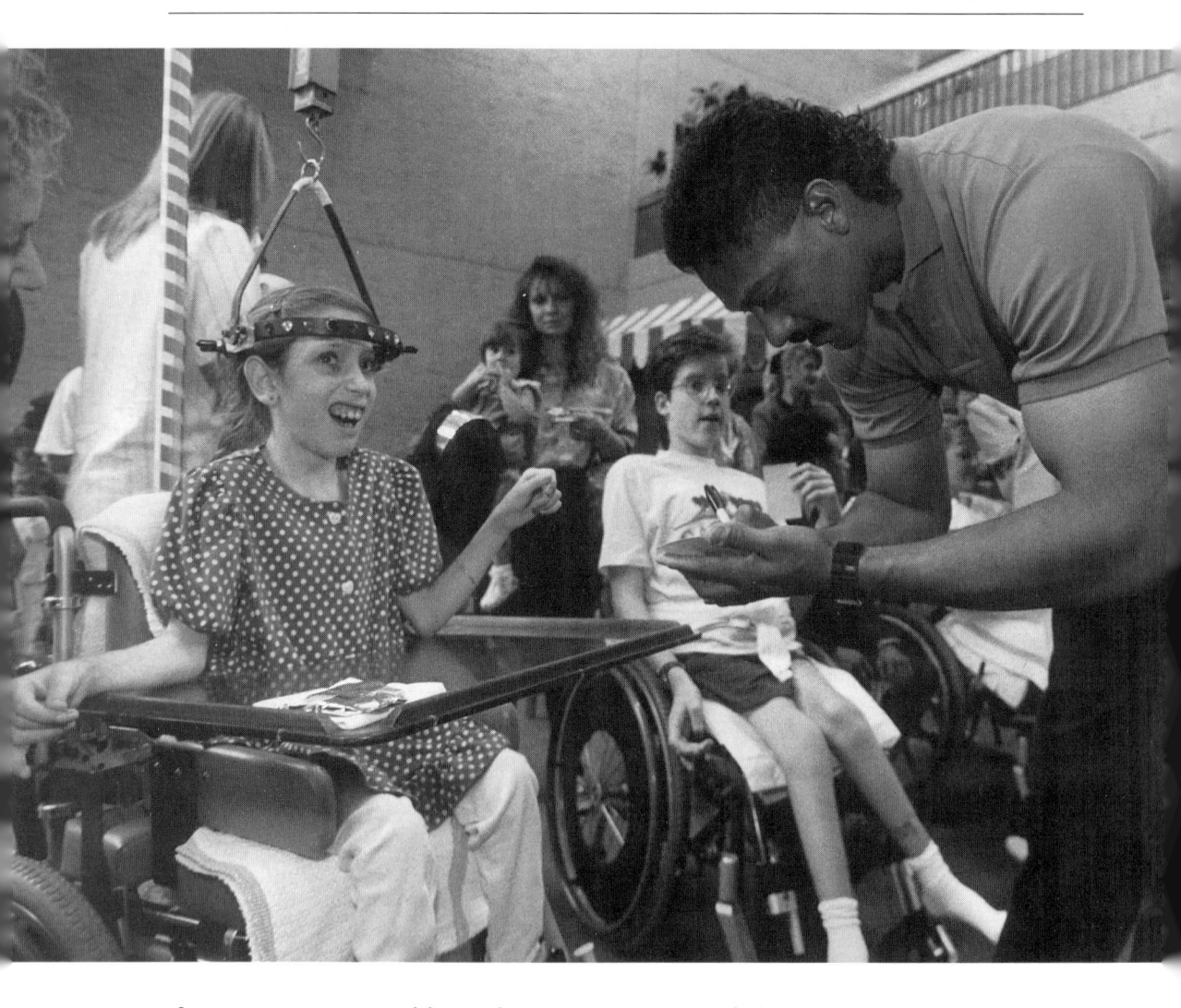

"We never saw that side because it had never been available to us," said Rangers general manager Tom Grieve. "One of the unfortunate things Latin players

Gonzalez autographs baseball cards for young patients at the Scottish Rite Hospital in Irving, Texas. "Many Latin American players close themselves in," Rangers scout Luis Rosa observed. "Juan is different. He is one who has understood the importance of both worlds."

face when they first get [into pro baseball] is the fact that they can't communicate through our language. Those of us who don't speak Spanish very well don't get to know them, which leads to stereotyping. Juan is bright. He's well-read. He's educated. He's sensitive. He's the same as a lot of players who speak English. The public just never knew it."

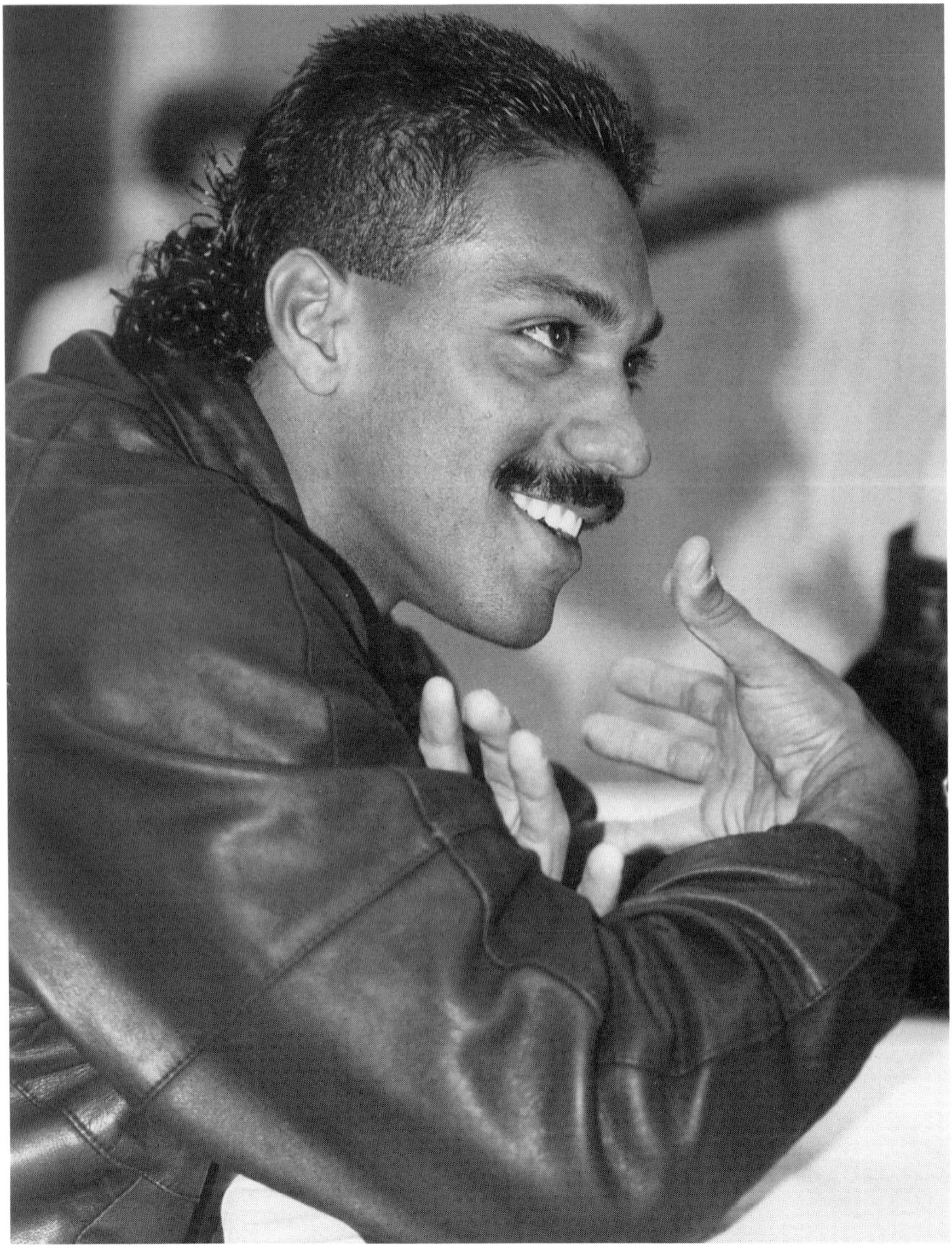

CHAPTER EIGHT

DESTINED FOR COOPERSTOWN?

Unlike Ken Griffey, Jr., Juan Gonzalez is fascinated by the history of baseball. In January 1993, he traveled to Baltimore to accept the prestigious Babe Ruth Crown for being the 1992 home run champion. During his stay he toured the Babe Ruth Birthplace, a museum with many artifacts and pictures relating to the most famous home run hitter of all time.

Gonzalez was quickly recognized at the museum, and other visitors started to ask for his autograph. As usual, he could not refuse their requests. The museum finally found him a chair, and what was supposed to be a simple tour turned out to be a 90-minute autograph session for about 300 people. "I was proud because I was sitting in the home of Babe Ruth," he said.

Gonzalez appreciates the emphasis fans place on baseball history. He also understands the obstacles that confront him as baseball writers and fans compare his early-career accomplishments with some of the game's all-time greats. Only five other players had as many homers as Gonzalez at the same stage of their careers. Four of them—Mel Ott, Eddie Mathews, Frank Robinson, and Mickey Mantle—are already in the Hall of Fame. If Gonzalez and Griffey, the fifth player on the list, are to reach Cooperstown, they will have to overcome powerful odds.

Baseball history is filled with stories of players who started with great promise but never reached their full

An exuberant Gonzalez talks with reporters at Arlington Stadium in February 1994, after signing a $45 million contract with the Rangers. The pact elevated Gonzalez to the top 10 on the major league salary list.

potential. Tony Conigliaro is probably the saddest story. The young Boston Red Sox outfielder had 94 home runs by his 22nd birthday. But in 1967, when he was well on his way to a 30–home run season, he was hit in the eye by a pitch. Conigliaro finished with 20 home runs that year, but he struggled with headaches, double vision, and a fear of the ball for the remainder of his career. He retired in 1975 at age 30 with just 166 career home runs.

Further examples were provided by Roger Maris in the 1960s, Bob Horner in the 1970s and 1980s, and Darryl Strawberry in the 1980s and 1990s. They each had the talent to reach 500 home runs and take their place among the immortals. But injuries and other factors kept them from greatness. Horner hit 148 home runs in his first five seasons with the Atlanta Braves, but a wrist injury forced him to retire after 11 seasons with just 248 career homers. Strawberry had 280 home runs by his 30th birthday, but injuries and drug problems limited him to just 10 homers between 1992 and 1994.

Maris achieved lasting fame when he broke Babe Ruth's single-season mark of 60 home runs by clouting 61 in 1961. At that time he was 27 years old and already had 186 career homers. Over the next three years he hit 82 more home runs, but then his career began to fade. Maris hit only 35 home runs over his final four seasons, and he retired after the 1968 season at age 34 with just 275 career homers.

Trying to avoid the fate of Horner, Maris, and Strawberry, among many others through time, Gonzalez rarely skips his workouts, and he prepares for each game as though it could be his last. "I could get hurt. I could never play baseball again," he has often reflected, thinking of his good friend Orlando Cepeda, who would have surely had 500 home runs if not for his constant knee injuries.

The Yankees' Roger Maris hits a high fly ball in 1961, the historic year in which he broke Babe Ruth's single-season home run record. Unfortunately, Maris's production declined after 1964, and he failed to achieve the numbers necessary for election to the Hall of Fame.

The ticket to Cooperstown is not just home run power but also preparation and consistency. The great home run hitters did not reach the Hall of Fame by hitting 50 home runs for 10 straight years. Instead, they hit 30 or more over 17, 18, 19, or even 20 seasons, with a couple of truly big years thrown in. To do that a player has to stay healthy. Hank Aaron is the classic example.

Not until his fourth season, in 1957, did Aaron's line drives start finding the seats. His highest home run total in any given season was 44. In addition to his record 755 career homers, he finished with a .305 lifetime batting average, a remarkable figure for a modern power hitter. Aaron excelled in every aspect of the game and never stopped learning. But the key to his accomplishment lies in the fact that he played 23 seasons without a major injury. He played 140 or more games a year 16 times.

Likewise, Gonzalez knows that staying healthy is the key to his eventual place in baseball history. By the time he reached age 24, he was averaging a home run every 15 at-bats while playing in an average of

150 games per year. At that ratio (at 500 at-bats per season) he was projected to have 521 home runs by the year 2005. That would place him 10th on the all-time list, tied with Hall of Famers Ted Williams and Willie McCovey.

When Gonzalez was told that the most homers Aaron ever hit in a season was 44, he was astonished. "Wow," he exclaimed. "He was Mr. Consistency, like Teddy Williams. That's a lot of years hitting over 30 home runs. Those are real numbers. Do you know how many people in baseball history never lived up to it? Those are very real numbers over a long, long time."

Like Aaron, Gonzalez rarely took himself out of the lineup. But he was often guilty of putting too much pressure on himself to satisfy the high expectations of others. In 1994, for example, he caught himself constantly swinging for the fences on almost every

Frank Thomas of the Chicago White Sox admires one of his home runs in 1993. Thomas, Gonzalez, and Ken Griffey, Jr., have established themselves as the American League's premier sluggers for the 1990s and beyond.

pitch—even when the pitch could not possibly be hit for a home run. When the two-time defending home run champion had only 11 homers at the end of June, he worried that the people of Puerto Rico and baseball experts would consider him a "flash in the pan."

As it turned out, 1994 became a year Gonzalez would rather forget. He started off slowly, which he usually does because, as he explained, "it's very hard for me to get used to the cold weather after being in the warm weather of Puerto Rico and Florida." Then, his brother's death affected him deeply. He also made many appearances at charity events and baseball card shows to meet the demands of the public. In addition, he had to cope with the Rangers' beautiful new stadium, the Ballpark in Arlington, Texas.

Gonzalez had greatly anticipated playing in the sparkling new stadium—until he saw the massive distances of the fences: 334 feet in left field, with a 14-foot-high fence; 388 in left-center field, where he usually hits most of his home runs; and 400 to straightaway center field. "I wondered why they built such a big field," he said. "The other players were wondering, too. A lot of times [in Arlington Stadium] I'd hit balls that were fly-outs and I thought once we moved from the other stadium I'd hit more home runs."

Thus, with the new contract, the new stadium, and the expectations of his followers in the Hispanic community came new pressures. Gonzalez began slowly, but he was starting to come around when the season was ended on August 12 by a players' strike. He finished with 19 home runs, 85 RBI, and a .275 average. Projected over a complete season, his statistics would have been 28 homers and 121 RBI—still an outstanding year for most players.

"I made the mistake of trying too much for hitting homers, trying to pull everything," Gonzalez said.

"My average went down, my homers were down." However, he felt he learned a valuable lesson from his troubling year. "I tried too hard, tried to do too much," he said. "I tried so hard. Early in the year my mind wasn't in the game. There was too much pressure. And I'm young, too. I'm a young man. That's a big point. I'm still learning things."

Gonzalez has admitted the pressure on him is often greater than that on contemporaries such as Griffey and Chicago's Frank Thomas. "There are few Latin American heroes," he once said. "We're a motivation and inspiration to so many young ones back home. They can see there are other ways to live than to get lost in drugs and other negatives in life. I have to do my best to prove to the youth that hard work can accomplish anything.... Pressure does exist. It comes from the fans, it comes from the media, and it comes

Gonzalez relaxes with his son, Juan Igor, before a Rangers game in 1994. Gonzalez has long appreciated the value of a proper upbringing: "I had a good home, where morals played a very important role," he recalled proudly.

from myself. I deal with it by simply doing the best I can every day. All I want is for God to give me good health so I can do the best. I'm not here to break records, I'm just here to give my best and see what happens."

Griffey's comment on the subject of pressure was, "I don't even think about that stuff." Nevertheless, the pressure for home run hitters to produce can be overwhelming. In baseball terms, a home run is no more important than pitching a shutout, stealing a base, or making a big play in the field. But there is nothing more dramatic than a home run, and fans have a special love for home run hitters. Babe Ruth remains the most popular baseball player ever. He led the majors in home runs 12 of the 14 years between 1918 and 1931, and he did it with style, enjoying seasons of 54, 55, 59, and 60 home runs. As Aaron closed in on Ruth's all-time home run mark of 714 in 1974, the entire world watched and waited with fascination. The record-shattering blow was carried on national TV and replayed countless times on news broadcasts.

Gonzalez clearly has the ability to create similar excitement. But the key to putting up big career numbers depends on his batting average, his ability to make better contact, and his continuing to mature. A player hitting 45 home runs and batting .230 can be pitched to; his low average suggests that there are "holes" in his style, areas where pitchers can spot the ball and turn him into an easy out. Players with higher batting averages usually mature as power hitters. Gonzalez took note. A lifetime .259 hitter before 1993, he batted .310 in 1993 and still posted a remarkable .632 slugging percentage.

While the media constantly speculate about Gonzalez's ability to hit 50 homers in a season, it has never been a big issue with him. Aaron never did it, nor did Ott, Robinson, or Mathews. In Gonzalez's view, 50 is nothing more than a number. "Fifty is not that important," he has said, deflecting talk of the Hall of Fame and comparison to some of the game's greatest power hitters. "Forty-six ties the mark of Puerto Rican players—Cepeda [in 1961]. Forty-seven ties the mark of Latin Americans—George Bell [in 1987]. And 48 will put me number one. Fifty home runs isn't impossible. It's difficult but it's not impossible. I would like to do it. But if I don't, I will walk away happy with what I've done."

As for his goals, he sets them each year but keeps them private. A close friend once said that Gonzalez wanted to retire with a .300 batting average, 500 home runs, and 2,000 RBI. Of course, most major leaguers would like those career statistics, as well. If

Gonzalez high-fives Dean Palmer after a home run in 1993. Reflecting on Gonzalez's future in baseball, Orlando Cepeda said, "Hit 500 home runs? Try 600. This is only the beginning for him."

Gonzalez were to post those numbers he would certainly be assured a place in the Hall of Fame.

Gonzalez admits that his goal is to one day reach Cooperstown. But it is also his goal to make life for Puerto Ricans more pleasant, to stop drug use on the streets, to inspire children to get an education, and to give the people of his homeland a vision for a brighter future. In some ways, he gives the impression that these things are more important to him than his own success on the baseball field. "Many of the kids I knew had trouble with the law. Some died. Some went to jail," he once observed. "That led me on a mission of sending the message out: get a good education, live life right, and good things will happen for you."

Many people think Gonzalez delivers his message by simply being on a baseball field. Gonzalez, Carlos Baerga, Roberto and Sandy Alomar, and other Puerto Ricans in the major leagues serve as inspirations to their people. The players' successes give the children of the island a realistic dream: anything can be accomplished with hard work, dedication, and a positive attitude.

"Fame and money does not make me a different person," Gonzalez has said. "I consider myself fortunate for the way I was brought up. My father worked two jobs, and my mother worked in the factory at General Electric in Vega Baja for some time. They both worked very hard, and I learned to appreciate their efforts. I had a good home, where morals played a very important role."

Other players marvel at Gonzalez's dedication and determination. "He's the kind of guy who you'll look back on and say, 'It was an honor playing with him,'" said Rangers third baseman Dean Palmer. "I'm talking about Hall of Fame caliber. He's that special."

But Gonzalez is not thinking about the Hall of Fame yet. His work, on and off the field, is far from being done.

APPENDIX: COMPARATIVE STATISTICS

YOUNGEST HOME RUN CHAMPIONS

Player	Year	HR	Birthdate
TONY CONIGLIARO, Boston Red Sox	1965	32	Jan. 7, 1945
SAM CRAWFORD, Cincinnati Reds	1901	16	April 18, 1880
EDDIE MATHEWS, Milwaukee Braves	1953	47	Oct. 13, 1931
TY COBB, Detroit Tigers	1909	9	Dec. 18, 1886
JOE DIMAGGIO, New York Yankees	1937	46	Nov. 25, 1914
JOHNNY BENCH, Cincinnati Reds	1970	45	Dec. 7, 1947
JUAN GONZALEZ, Texas Rangers	1992	43	Oct. 16, 1969

YOUNGEST PLAYERS TO HAVE THREE 100-RBI SEASONS

Player	Years	Birthdate
MEL OTT, New York Giants	1929–31	March 2, 1909
TY COBB, Detroit Tigers	1907–9	Dec. 18, 1886
TED WILLIAMS, Boston Red Sox	1939–41	Aug. 30, 1918
JOE DIMAGGIO, New York Yankees	1936–38	Nov. 25, 1914
KEN GRIFFEY, JR., Seattle Mariners	1991–93	Nov. 21, 1969
JUAN GONZALEZ, Texas Rangers	1991–93	Oct. 16, 1969

PLAYERS WITH MOST CAREER HOME RUNS BY AGE 24

Player	HR
EDDIE MATHEWS, Milwaukee Braves	153
MEL OTT, New York Giants	153
KEN GRIFFEY, JR., Seattle Mariners	132
FRANK ROBINSON, Cincinnati Reds	130
MICKEY MANTLE, New York Yankees	121
JUAN GONZALEZ, Texas Rangers	21

CHRONOLOGY

1969	Born Juan Alberto Gonzalez Vazquez on October 16 in Vega Baja, Puerto Rico
1985	Signs professional contract with the Texas Rangers
1986	Begins professional career with Sarasota Rangers in the Gulf Coast League; leads the league in RBI
1987	Promoted to Gastonia in the South Atlantic (Sally) League; bats .265 with 14 home runs and 74 RBI
1988	Bats .256 with 8 home runs and 43 RBI during 80-game season with Charlotte in the Florida State League
1989	Plays minor league season with Tulsa in the Texas League; promoted to Texas Rangers for final month of the American League season; hits first major league home run on September 18
1990	Plays his final season in the minors with Oklahoma City of the American Association; hits 29 home runs and drives in 101 runs; plays 25 games with the Rangers in September, batting .289 with 4 home runs and 12 RBI

1991	Plays first full major league season; bats .264 with 27 home runs and 102 RBI
1992	Marries Jackie Ortiz; wins American League home run title with 43; son, Juan Igor, is born
1993	Wins All-Star Game home run–hitting contest; hits 100th career home run; bats .310 for the season and repeats as American League home run champion
1994	Signs seven-year, $45 million contract with the Rangers; begins campaign to build a sports center in Vega Baja and creates a youth foundation

FURTHER READING

Cepeda, Orlando, with Bob Markus. *High and Inside—Orlando Cepeda's Story.* South Bend, IN: B L Publishers, 1984.

Clark, Brooks. "Juan's World." *Sports Illustrated for Kids,* April 1994.

Fraley, Jerry. "A Higher Calling." *Dallas Morning News,* January 30, 1994.

Gilbert, Thomas W. *Roberto Clemente.* New York: Chelsea House, 1991.

Horn, Barry. "Living the Life of a Can't-Miss Prospect." *Dallas Morning News,* July 27, 1986.

James, Bill. *The Bill James Player Ratings.* New York: Collier, 1994.

Lawes, Rick, and Milton Jamail. "Igor." *USA Today Baseball Weekly,* September 15, 1993.

Mills, David. "Mighty Gonzalez at Bat." *Washington Post,* August 23, 1993.

Oleksak, Michael M., and Mary Adams Oleksak. *Béisbol: Latin Americans and the Grand Old Game.* Indianapolis, IN: Masters Press, 1991.

Robbins, Danny. "Gonzalez Bridges Two Worlds." *Los Angeles Times,* June 20, 1993.

Sullivan, T. R. "Powerful Influence." *Fort Worth Star-Telegram,* September 10, 1993.

Thorn, John, and Pete Palmer. *Total Baseball.* 3rd ed. New York: HarperCollins, 1993.

Tuttle, Dennis. "Juan Gonzalez: Next Home Run King." *Tuff Stuff,* March 1994.

Vass, George, with Jose Cruz. "The Game I'll Never Forget." *Baseball Digest,* December 1985.

Verducci, Tom. "Puerto Rico's New Patron Saint." *Sports Illustrated,* April 14, 1993.

INDEX

Aaron, Hank, 97, 98, 101, 102
Alianza para un Puerto Rico Sin Drogas (Alliance for a Puerto Rico Without Drugs), 88
All-Star Game, 1993, 15–18, 82
Alomar, Roberto, 24, 37, 45, 90, 103
Alomar, Sandy, Jr., 24, 37, 90, 103
Alvarez, Wilson, 64, 66
American League, 18, 53, 73, 82
Associated Press Major League All-Star Team, 83
Babe Ruth Crown, 95
Baerga, Carlos, 24, 25, 37, 39, 44, 45, 90, 103
Baines, Harold, 65, 66
Baseball Hall of Fame, 95, 97, 102, 103
Baseball Weekly, 18, 20
Béisbol: Latin Americans and the Grand Old Game (Oleksak and Oleksak), 35
Bell, George, 102
Bithorn, Hiram, 27–28, 29
Bonds, Barry, 16, 82

Cadahia, Chino, 57, 59, 61, 63, 64
Canel, Buck, 30, 33
Caribbean World Series, 29
Carolina, Puerto Rico, 36
Carolina League, 61
Cepeda, Orlando, 20, 23, 24, 26, 31–32, 39, 77, 86, 90, 96, 102
Cepeda, Perucho, 26, 31
Ciudad Deportiva (Sports City), 36
Clemens, Roger, 65
Clemente, Roberto, 20, 23, 24, 31, 32–34, 35–36, 37, 42, 83, 86, 91
Conigliaro, Tony, 96
Cruz, Jose, 37, 42, 43–44
Cuba, 27, 28, 29, 30, 31
Darling, Ron, 66
DiMaggio, Joe, 82
Dominican Republic, 25, 30
Escalara, Nino, 31
Figueroa, Ed, 37
Florida State League, 63–64
Franco, Julio, 69
Gibson, Josh, 26
Gomez, Leo, 90
Gomez, Orlando, 45, 76, 81
Gomez, Ruben, 31

Gonzalez, Jackie Ortiz (wife), 78
Gonzalez, Juan, Sr. (father), 40, 41, 42, 46, 47, 72, 80, 86, 91, 103
Gonzalez, Juan
   All-Star Game home run–hitting contest, 1993, 15–18, 82
   American League home run titles, 18–19, 23, 24, 76–77, 95
   awards, 83, 95
   and Baseball Hall of Fame, 95–103
   birth, 39
   charity work, 83, 85–92, 103
   childhood, 39–47
   education, 44
   fame in Puerto Rico, 20–21, 23, 24, 77, 86, 90–91
   language barrier, 18, 34, 54–56, 60, 61, 70, 74, 79, 93
   major league career, 67, 69–71, 72–102
   marriage, 78
   minor league career, 49–67, 72
   professional contract, signs, 39, 47
   United States, adjusts to, 35, 49–56, 63
   and winter ball, 64, 71, 86, 90

Gonzalez, Juan Igor (son), 40, 78
Gonzalez, Lelé (mother), 40, 42, 47, 52, 63, 72, 80, 85, 91, 103
Gonzalez Roman, Juan Alberto (stepbrother), 42, 85, 86
Grieve, Tom, 18, 21, 53, 92
Griffey, Ken, Jr., 15, 16, 17, 18, 82, 95, 100, 101
Gulf Coast League, 49
Guzman, Jose, 72
Harrah, Toby, 79, 80
Horner, Bob, 96
Instructional league, 56, 59
Jackson, Reggie, 77
Jaramillo, Rudy, 50, 51, 52, 54, 56, 60, 63, 64
Johnson, Sandy, 39, 53, 56
Kennedy, Kevin, 34, 80
Knoblauch, Chuck, 73, 74
Latin America, 20, 27, 37, 47, 55, 59, 63
McCovey, Willie, 98
McGwire, Mark, 76, 77
Mantle, Mickey, 77, 95, 96
Maris, Roger, 96
Marquez, Luis, 28
Martinez, Edgar, 90
Mathews, Eddie, 95, 102
Mattingly, Don, 77
Mayoral, Luis, 19, 20, 24, 37, 80, 81
Mays, Willie, 30, 31, 34
Mexican League, 28
Mickey Mantle League, 45

INDEX

Montanez, Willie, 37
National League, 23, 28, 82
Olmo, Luis, 28
Ott, Mel, 82, 95, 102
Paige, Satchel, 26
Palmeiro, Rafael, 69, 70, 74, 79
Palmer, Dean, 49, 51, 54, 59, 61, 63, 67, 102
Perez, Tony, 31
Ponce Lions, 44
Power, Vic, 31, 45
Puerto Rican League, 26
Puerto Rico, 15, 20, 21, 36, 37, 40, 45, 47, 55, 59, 60, 72, 77, 89, 90, 99, 103
   baseball, 23–31
   winter league baseball, 31, 36, 45, 55, 64, 71, 86, 90
Racism, 27, 28, 29, 33, 60
Rio Piedras, Puerto Rico, 69
Robinson, Frank, 95, 102
Robinson, Jackie, 29
Robson, Tom, 67, 69, 70, 71, 72, 75, 76, 79
Rodriguez, Ivan, 37, 44, 45, 67, 69
Rookie league, 49, 53
Rosa, Luis, 39, 42, 47
Ruth, Babe, 42, 95, 96, 101
Ryan, Nolan, 18, 19, 74, 75, 83
Sanchez, Rey, 49
San Juan, Puerto Rico, 23, 40
Santurce, Puerto Rico, 27
Santurce Cangrejeros, 31

Sarasota Rangers, 49
Sierra, Ruben, 37, 69
Sixto Escobar Stadium, 26
Sosa, Sammy, 49, 51, 53, 54, 59, 60, 61, 63, 64, 65, 66, 74
South Atlantic (Sally) League, 59, 60, 61
Sporting News, The, 37
   American League All-Star Team, 83
Sports Illustrated, 19, 20, 39, 88, 92
Strawberry, Darryl, 96
Terrell, Walt, 66
Texas Rangers, 15, 18, 19, 20, 37, 39, 45, 46, 47, 49, 51, 53, 54, 56, 57, 59, 63, 65, 66, 67, 69, 71, 72, 73, 76, 77, 78, 79, 80, 81, 83, 88, 92, 99, 103
Thomas, Frank, 77, 99
Thompson, Tommy, 64
United States, 24, 25, 28, 30, 36, 49, 74, 80, 91
Valentine, Bobby, 69, 71, 72, 74, 78, 92
Vega Baja, Puerto Rico, 39, 40, 42, 55, 69, 86, 103
Venezuela, 29, 55
Williams, Bernie, 45
Williams, Ted, 98
Winfield, Dave, 42
Winter league baseball, 23, 26, 29, 31, 36, 45, 55, 64, 71, 86, 90
"Yo Sí Puedo" (Yes I Can) educational program, 88

DENNIS R. TUTTLE, a native of North Carolina, began his sportswriting career at age 17 at his hometown paper, the Winston-Salem *Journal,* in 1977. He has also been a writer and editor at the Cincinnati *Enquirer,* Austin *American-Statesman,* Knoxville *Journal,* and Washington *Times.* A 1982 graduate of the University of Cincinnati, he is a two-time winner of the Associated Press Sports Editor's Award for sportswriting excellence. He resides in Alexandria, Virginia.

RODOLFO CARDONA is professor of Spanish and comparative literature at Boston University. A renowned scholar, he has written many works of criticism, including *Ramón, a Study of Gómez de la Serna and His Works* and *Visión del esperpento: Teoría y práctica del esperpento en Valle-Inclán.* Born in San José, Costa Rica, he earned his B.A. and M.A. from Louisiana State University and received a Ph.D. from the University of Washington. He has taught at Case Western Reserve University, the University of Pittsburgh, the University of Texas at Austin, the University of New Mexico, and Harvard University.

JAMES COCKCROFT is currently a visiting professor of Latin American and Caribbean studies at the State University of New York at Albany. A three-time Fulbright scholar, he earned a Ph.D. from Stanford University and has taught at the University of Massachusetts, the University of Vermont, and the University of Connecticut. He is the author or coauthor of numerous books on Latin American subjects, including *Neighbors in Turmoil: Latin America, The Hispanic Experience in the United States: Contemporary Issues and Perspectives,* and *Outlaws in the Promised Land: Mexican Immigrant Workers and America's Future.*

PICTURE CREDITS

AP/Wide World Photos: pp. 14, 25, 32, 48, 55, 57, 68, 84, 94; Courtesy Louis DeLuca, the *Dallas Morning News*: p. 78; Courtesy Frank H. Fleer Co.: p. 62 (top left); Courtesy Gonzalez family: p. 41; Courtesy Mitchell Haddad: pp. 38, 81; National Baseball Library, Cooperstown, NY: p. 27; Reuters/Bettmann: pp. 17, 75, 98, 102; Courtesy John F. Rhodes, the *Dallas Morning News*: p. 92; Courtesy Bill Speer, *Sarasota Herald-Tribune*/Silver Image: p. 53; Courtesy Texas Rangers: pp. 50, 65, 70, 73, 87, 89, 100; Courtesy the Topps Company Inc.: p. 62; UPI/Bettmann: 19, 22, 34, 37, 43, 46, 58, 97.